FILMED BOOKS AND PLAYS 1975-1981

FILMED BOOKS
AND PLAYS

A LIST OF BOOKS AND PLAYS
FROM WHICH FILMS HAVE BEEN
MADE, 1975-81

by
A. G. S. ENSER, FLA, FRSA

Gower

A Grafton Book

Published by
Gower Publishing Company Limited
Gower House
Croft Road
Aldershot
Hampshire GU11 3HR

Distributed in the United States and Canada by

Lexington Books
D.C. Heath & Company
125 Spring Street
Lexington
Massachusetts 02173

British Library Cataloguing in Publication Data

Enser, A.G.S.
    Filmed books and plays : a list of books and plays
    from which films have been made, 1975—81.
    1. Film adaptations — Bibliography
    I. Title
    011'.37   Z5784.M9

    ISBN 0 566 03475 1

Printed and bound in Great Britain by
Biddles Ltd, Guildford and King's Lynn

CONTENTS

v

PREFACE

Scope

This is a Supplement to *Filmed Books and Plays 1928–1974*. It includes films made from books and plays during 1975 to 1981, and also omissions from the previous volume.

Altogether, approximately 580 new and changed titles are added, together with 380 author entries.

Arrangement

There are three indexes, namely:

   (a)   Film Title Index
   (b)   Author Index
   (c)   Change of Original Title Index

The articles 'The', 'A' or 'An' are placed at the end of the title instead of at the beginning and are ignored in alphabetical arrangement. The Film Title Index is arranged alphabetically under the title of the film. Underneath is shown the name of the maker or distributing company (usually in abbreviation) and the year the film was made.

Opposite is shown the name of the author of the book from which the film was made and underneath, the name of the publisher.

Where another title, in italics, follows the name of the author, this signifies that the film company changed the title of the book from the original shown in italics to that printed opposite.

Where (P) is found, this signifies that the book is in play form. The Author Index is arranged alphabetically under the names of the authors with further alphabetical arrangement under each author of his works which have been filmed. Underneath the title of the work filmed is shown the name of the publisher.

Opposite is shown the name of the maker or distributing company. Should a title in italics follow, this signifies the title under which the film was presented. It will be noted that in this index liberty has been taken to use an author's pseudonym.

The Change of Original Title Index is an alphabetical arrangement of original book titles differing from their film titles. Underneath the original book title is found the name of the author. Opposite is found the title of the film with underneath the name of the maker or distributing company and the relevant year.

How to use the Indexes

If the name of the film is known, but not the name of the author of the book, refer to the Film Title Index.

Ignore any article 'The', 'A' or 'An'.

If the name of the author is known, but not that of the book or film, refer to the Author Index where under the author's name will be found, in alphabetical arrangement, the titles of his works which have been filmed.

If it is desired to know which works of a particular author have been filmed, refer to the Author Index.

If the original title of the book is known but not that given to the film, nor is the author's name known, refer to the Change of Original Title Index.

I shall be grateful to be informed of any errors or omissions.

A.G.S. ENSER
Eastbourne
JULY 1982

viii

LIST OF ABBREVIATIONS

AA	Anglo-Amalgamated Film Company
AB	Associated British Film Distributors
ABP	Associated British and Pathe Film Distributors
ALL	Alliance Productions Ltd
ARC	The Archers Film Productions Ltd
AUT	Auten Films
BD	British and Dominion Films Ltd
BI	British International Films
BL	British Lion Films Ltd
BN	British National Films Ltd
CFF	Children's Film Foundation
CIN	Cineguild Incorporated
CIC	Cinema International Corporation
CIN	Cineguild Incorporated
COL	Columbia Productions Ltd
CONT	Continental Films Ltd
EAL	Ealing Studios Ltd
EL	Eagle Lion Distributors Ltd
EMI	Thorn EMI Films
FOX	Fox and Twentieth Century Fox Ltd
GB	Gaumont British Ltd
GFD	General Film Distributors Ltd
GTO	GTO Films
GUO	GUO Film Distributors
ID	First Division Films
IN	International Motion Pictures

ITC	ITC Film Distribution
jt. author	*joint author*
LF	London Films
MGM	Metro-Goldwyn-Mayer Ltd
MON	Monogram Films
OLY	Olympic Films
PAR	Paramount Productions Ltd
pseud	*pseudonym*
PRC	Producers' Releasing Corporation
RANK	J. Arthur Rank Film Distribution
REN	Renown Pictures Corporation Ltd
REP	Republic Pictures
RKO	R.K.O. Radio Pictures Ltd
SF	SAFIR Films
TC	Two Cities Films Ltd
UA	United Artists' Corporation
UI	Universal International Motion Pictures
UN	Universal Motion Pictures Ltd
WAR	Warner Brothers Pictures Ltd
WW	World Wide Films Ltd

FILM TITLE INDEX

A

ABBESS, THE
SCOTIA-BARBER 1976

Spark, Muriel, *(Abbess of Crewe, The)*
N.Y. Viking

ABDICATION, THE
COL—WAR 1974

Wolff, Ruth. (P)
Paperback Library

ABDUCTION
HEMDALE 1977

James, Harrison
N.Y. Whirlwind

ACES HIGH
EMI 1976

Sherriff, R.C. *(Journey's End)*
Gollancz

AGATHA
COL—EMI—WAR 1979

Christie, Agatha, *(And Then There Were None)*, Collins

AGENCY
CAROLCO 1980

Gottlieb, Paul
Sphere

AKINFIELD
ANGLE FILMS 1975

Blythe, Ronald
Penguin

ALICE
HEMDALE 1980

Carroll, Lewis, *(Alice in Wonderland)*
Various

ALL CREATURES GREAT AND SMALL
EMI 1974

Herriot, James, *(If Only They Could Talk : It Shouldn't Happen to a Vet)*, Joseph

ALL QUIET ON THE WESTERN FRONT
ITC 1980

Remarque, Erich M.
Putnam

ALL THE PRESIDENT'S MEN
COL—WAR 1976

Bernstein, C. *and* Woodward, R.
Secker & Warburg

ALTERED STATES
COL 1981

Chayefsky, Paddy
N.Y. Harper

AMERICAN FRIEND, THE
CINEGATE 1978

Highsmith, Patricia
Hodder & Stoughton

AMITYVILLE HORROR, THE
AMERICAN INTERNATIONAL 1979

Anson, Jay
N.Y. Bantam

ANTAGONISTS, THE
UA 1980

Gann, Ernest K. (U.S. title: *Masada)*
N.Y. New American Library

1

TITLE OF FILM	AUTHOR AND PUBLISHER
APPLE DUMPLING GANG, THE DISNEY 1974	Bickham, Jack M. Hale
APPRENTICESHIP OF DUDDY KRAVITZ, THE RANK 1975	Richler, Mordecai Deutsch
ASHANTI COL–EMI 1979	Vasquez-Figueroa, Alberto, *(Ebano)* Hale
AT THE EARTH'S CORE BL 1976	Burroughs, Edgar R. N.Y. Ace
AUDREY ROSE UA 1977	De Felitta, Frank Collins
AUTOBIOGRAPHY OF MISS JANE PITTMAN, THE SAGA 1975	Gaines, E.J. Bantam
AVALANCHE EXPRESS FOX 1979	Forbes, Colin N.Y. Dutton
AWAKENING, THE COL–EMI–WAR 1980	Stoker, Bram. *(Jewel of the Seven Stars)* Jarrolds

B

BAWDY ADVENTURES OF TOM JONES, THE CIC 1976	Fielding, Henry, *(Tom Jones)* Various
BEAR ISLAND COL–EMI–WAR 1979	MacLean, Alistair Collins
BEARS AND I, THE DISNEY 1974	Leslie, Robert F. N.Y. Ballantine
BEING THERE ITC 1980	Kosinski, Jerzy N.Y. Bantam
BELL JAR, THE AVCO EMBASSY 1978	Plath, Sylvia N.Y. Harper

2

TITLE OF FILM	AUTHOR AND PUBLISHER
BETSY, THE UA 1978	Robbins, Harold New English Library
BEYOND REASONABLE DOUBT J & M FILMS 1980	Yallop, David Hodder & Stoughton
BEYOND THE POSEIDON ADVENTURE COL–EMI–WAR 1979	Gallico, Paul Joseph
BIG FIX, THE CIC 1979	Simon, Roger L. N.Y. Pocket Books
BIG SLEEP, THE ITC 1978	Chandler, Raymond Hamilton
BIG STICK UP AT BRINKS UN 1979	Behn, Noel, *(Brink's Job, The)* N.Y. Putnam
BINGO LONG TRAVELLING ALL-STARS AND MOTOR KINGS, THE CIC 1976	Brashler, William N.Y. Harper
BITCH, THE BRENT WALKER 1979	Collins, Jackie Pan
BLACK BIRD, THE COL–WAR 1975	Hammett, Dashiel, *(Maltese Falcon, The)*, Cassell
BLACK EYE COL–WAR 1973	Jacks, Jeff, *(Murder on the Wild Side)* N.Y. Fawcett
BLACK JACK ENTERPRISE 1980	Garfield, Leon Longmans
BLACK MARBLE, THE AVCO EMBASSY 1980	Wambaugh, Joseph N.Y. Dell
BLACK STALLION UA 1979	Farley, Walter N.Y. Random
BLACK SUNDAY PAR 1977	Harris, Thomas Hodder & Stoughton
BLOODBROTHERS COL–WAR 1978	Price, Richard N.Y. Bantam

TITLE OF FILM	AUTHOR AND PUBLISHER
BLOODLINE CIC 1979	Sheldon, Sidney N.Y. Morrow
BLOOD RELATIVES RANK 1978	McBain, Ed. Hamilton
BLUE BIRD, THE FOX 1976	Maeterlinck, Maurice. (P) Methuen
BLUE BLOOD NATIONWIDE 1974	Thynne, Alexander Sphere
BLUE FIN SOUTH AUSTRALIA FILM 1978	Thiele, Colin Collins
BLUE LAGOON, THE COL 1980	Stacpoole, H. de V. Various
BLUE NIGHT, THE BUTCHER 1973	Wambaugh, Joseph Joseph
BOBBY DEERFIELD COL–WAR 1977	Remarque, Erich M. *(Heaven has no Favourites)*, N.Y. Harcourt
BORN AGAIN AVCO EMBASSY 1979	Colson, Charles N.Y. Bantam
BOUND FOR GLORY UA 1977	Guthrie, Woody N.Y. Dutton
BOYS FROM BRAZIL, THE ITC 1978	Levin, Ira Joseph
BRASS TARGET MGM 1978	Nolan, Frederick, *(Algonquin Project, The)*, N.Y. Morrow
BREAKHEART PASS UA 1975	MacLean, Alistair Collins
BREAKOUT COL–WAR 1975	Asinof, C. *(Ten Second Jailbreak)*, Joseph
BRIDGE TOO FAR, A UA 1977	Ryan, Cornelius Hamilton
BUG PAR 1975	Page, Thomas, *(Hephaestus Plague, The)* Putnam

4

BURNT OFFERINGS
UA 1976

Marasco, Robert
Coronet

BUTLEY
SEVEN KINGS 1973

Gray, Simon. (P)
N.Y. Viking

BUTTERFLY
J & M FILMS 1981

Cain, James M.
N.Y. Random

C

CADDIE
HEMDALE 1976

Brink, Carol R. *(Caddie Woodlawn)*
Collier-Macmillan

CALIFORNIA SUITE
COL 1979

Simon, Neil. (P)
N.Y. Random

CANDLESHOE
DISNEY 1977

Innes, Michael, *(Christmas at Candle-shoe)*, Gollancz

CANNERY ROW
MGM 1981

Steinbeck, John
Heinemann

CARAVANS
BORDEAUX FILMS 1979

Michener, James A.
N.Y. Random

CARRIE
UA 1976

King, Stephen
New English Library

CAT AND THE CANARY, THE
GALA 1981

Willard, John. (P)
Hudson

CATTLE ANNIE AND LITTLE BRITCHES
HEMDALE 1980

Ward, Robert
N.Y. Ace

CHANT OF JIMMIE BLACKSMITH, THE
FOX 1979

Keneally, Thomas
Angus & Robertson

CHAPTER TWO
COL—EMI—WAR 1980

Simon, Neil. (P)
N.Y. Random

CHARLEY AND THE ANGEL
DISNEY 1974

Stanton, Will, *(Golden Evenings of Summer, The)*, N.Y. Lancer

CHARLIE MUGGIN
EUSTON FILMS 1979

Freemantle, Brian, *(Charlie M)*
N.Y. Doubleday

TITLE OF FILM	AUTHOR AND PUBLISHER
CHICKEN CHRONICLES, THE ALPHA 1980	Diamond, Paul N.Y. Dell
CHILDREN OF SANCHEZ, THE HALL BARTLETT 1978	Lewis, Oscar N.Y. Random
CHOIRBOYS, THE GTO 1977	Wambaugh, Joseph Weidenfeld & Nicolson
CIRCLE OF TWO BORDEAUX FILMS 1982	Baird, Marie-Therese, *(Lesson in Love, A)*, Various
CLASS OF MISS MacMICHAEL, THE GALA 1980	Hutson, Sandy, *(Eff Off)* Corgi
COAL MINER'S DAUGHTER UN 1980	Lynn, Loretta *and* Vecsey, George Warner
COCKFIGHTER EMI 1974	Willeford, Charles N.Y. Crown
COMA CIC 1978	Cook, Robin Boston: Little, Brown
CONDUCT UNBECOMING BL 1975	England, Barry. (P) French
CONFESSIONS FROM A HOLIDAY CAMP COL–WAR 1977	Lea, Timothy Sphere
CONFESSIONS OF A DRIVING INSTRUCTOR COL–WAR 1976	Lea, Timothy Sphere
CONFESSIONS OF A POP PERFORMER COL–WAR 1975	Lea, Timothy, *(Confessions from the Pop Scene),* Futura
CONFESSIONS OF A WINDOW CLEANER COL–WAR 1974	Lea, Timothy Futura
CONRACK FOX 1976	Conroy, Pat. *(Water is Wide, The)* N.Y. Dell
COUNT OF MONTE CRISTO, THE SCOTIA–BARBER 1976	Dumas, Alexandre Various

6

CRAZE EMI 1974	Seymour, Henry, *(Infernal Idol)* N.Y. Avon
CROKING ITC 1980	Walker, Gerald W.H. Allen
CROSSED SWORDS FOX 1977	Twain, Mark, *(Prince and the Pauper, The)* Various
CROSS OF IRON EMI 1976	Heinrich, Willi, *(Willing Flesh)* Corgi
CRUEL PASSION TARGET 1978	De Sade, *Marquis, (Justine)* Various
CUSTARD BOYS, THE FOREST HALL 1980	Rae, John Hart-Davis
CUTTER'S WAY UA 1981	Thornburg, Newton, *(Cutter and Bone)* Heinemann

D

DAISY MILLER CIC 1974	James, Henry Hart-Davis
DAMNATION ALLEY FOX 1978	Zelazny, Roger N.Y. Putnam
DANGEROUS DAVIES – THE LAST DETECTIVE INNER CIRCLE FILMS 1980	Thomas, Leslie Eyre & Methuen
DANGEROUS LOVE BRUT 1978	Christman, Elizabeth, *(Nice Italian Girl, A)*, N.Y. Dodd
DAY OF THE LOCUST, THE CIC 1975	West, Nathaniel N.Y. New Directions
DEATH ON THE NILE EMI 1978	Christie, Agatha Collins
DEATH SENTENCE CANNON 1981	Garfield, Brian Evans

TITLE OF FILM	AUTHOR AND PUBLISHER
DEATH WATCH CONTEMPORARY 1979	Compton, David, *(Continuous Katherine* *Mortenhoe, The)*, N.Y. Arrow
DEATH WISH CANNON 1981	Garfield, Brian Hodder & Stoughton
DEATH WISH II CANNON 1981	Garfield, Brian Hodder & Stoughton
DEEP, THE COL—WAR 1977	Benchley, Peter Deutsch
DEER HUNTER, THE COL—EMI 1979	Corder, E.M. Hodder & Stoughton
DELICATE BALANCE, A SEVEN KEYS 1974	Albee, Edward Cape
DEMON SEED MGM 1977	Koontz, Dean Toronto: Bantam
DESPAIR GALA 1978	Nabokov, Vladimir N.Y. Putnam
DEVIL'S ADVOCATE, THE RANK 1977	West, Morris Heinemann
DIRTY TRICKS FILMPLAN 1980	Gifford, Thomas, *(Glendower Legacy,* *The)*, Putnam
DISAPPEARANCE, THE CINEGATE 1977	Marlowe, Derek, *(Echoes of Celandine)* Penguin
DOC SAVAGE — THE MAN OF BRONZE COL—WAR 1975	Robeson, Kenneth Corgi
DOGS OF WAR, THE UA 1980	Forsyth, Frederick Hutchinson
DOG SOLDIERS UA 1978	Stone, Robert Secker & Warburg
DOMINO KILLINGS, THE ITC 1978	Kennedy, Adam, *(Domino Principle,* *The)*, N.Y. Viking
DONA FLOR AND HER TWO HUSBANDS FD 1978	Amado, Jorge N.Y. Avon

TITLE OF FILM	AUTHOR AND PUBLISHER
DON'T JUST LIE THERE, SAY SOMETHING RANK 1975	Pertwee, Michael. (P) French
DRACULA CIC 1979	Stoker, Bram. Various
DRACULA SUCKS KODIAK FILMS 1979	Stoker, Bram. *(Dracula)* Various
DROWNING POOL, THE COL–WAR 1975	Macdonald, Ross Fontana
DRUM PAR 1976	Onstott, Kyle Pan
DUBAI AMERICAN COMMUNICATION INDUSTRIES 1980	Moore, Robin N.Y. Doubleday
DUELLISTS, THE CIC 1977	Conrad, Joseph Fontana

E

EAGLE HAS LANDED, THE ITC 1976	Higgins, Jack Collins
ECLIPSE GALA 1976	Woolaston, Nicholas Macmillan
EIGER SANCTION, THE CIC 1975	Trevanian Heinemann
EMMANUELLE SF 1975	Arsan, Emmanuelle Mayflower
EMPIRE OF THE ANTS BRENT WALKER 1978	Wells, H.G., *(Valley of the Ants, The)* Fontana
ENDLESS LOVE BARBER 1981	Spencer, Scott N.Y. Knopf
END OF AUGUST, THE ENTERPRISE 1981	Chopin, Kate, *(Awakening, The)* N.Y. Avon

TITLE OF FILM	AUTHOR AND PUBLISHER
ENEMY OF THE PEOPLE, AN ENTERPRISE 1978	Ibsen, Henrik. (P) Various
ENIGMA FILMCREST 1981	Barak, Michael N.Y. New American Library
ENTERTAINER, THE SEVEN KEYS 1975	Osborne, John. (P) Evans
EQUUS UA 1977	Shaffer, Peter Deutsch
ESCAPE FROM ALCATRAZ CIC 1979	Bruce, J.C. N.Y. McGraw
ESCAPE TO WITCH MOUNTAIN DISNEY 1974	Key, Alexander Various
EVERY WHICH WAY BUT LOOSE COL–EMI–WAR 1980	Kronberg, Jeremy J. Hale
EVIL UNDER THE SUN COL 1981	Christie, Agatha Collins
EXCALIBUR COL–EMI–WAR 1981	Malory, *Sir* Thomas, *(Morte d'Arthur, Le),* Various
EYE OF THE NEEDLE UA 1981	Follett, Kenneth N.Y. New American Library

F

FAMILY PLOT UN 1976	Canning, Victor, *(Rainbird Pattern, The)* Heinemann
FAN, THE CIC 1981	Randall, Bob N.Y. Random
FAREWELL MY LOVELY FOX–RANK 1975	Chandler, Raymond Hamilton
FEDORA MAINLINE 1979	Tryon, Thomas, *(Crowned Heads)* N.Y. Fawcett

TITLE OF FILM	AUTHOR AND PUBLISHER
FIFTH MUSKETEER, THE SASCHA WIEN FILMS 1978	Dumas, Alexandre, *(Man in the Iron Mask, The),* Various
FINAL ACT, THE SAWBUCK 1980	Hudson, Christopher Joseph
FIRE SALE FOX 1978	Klane, Robert N.Y. Fawcett
FIRST DEADLY SIN, THE CIC 1981	Sanders, Lawrence N.Y. Macmillan
FIRST GREAT TRAIN ROBBERY, THE UA 1979	Crichton, Michael, *(Great Train Robbery The),* Cape
F.I.S.T. UA 1978	Eszterhas, Joe N.Y. Dell
FORCE 10 FROM NAVARONE COL–WAR 1978	MacLean, Alistair Collins
FORMULA, THE MGM 1980	Shagan, Steve N.Y. Bantam
FOR YOUR EYES ONLY UA 1981	Fleming, Ian Cape
FOUR FEATHERS, THE TRIDENT BARBER 1978	Mason, A.E.W. Hodder & Stoughton
FOUR MUSKETEERS, THE FOX–RANK 1974	Dumas, Alexandre, *(Three Musketeers)* Various
FOX AND THE HOUND DISNEY 1981	Mannix, Daniel Various
FRAMED CIC 1974	Powers, Art *and* Misenheimer, Mike Pinnacle
FREAKY FRIDAY DISNEY 1976	Rodgers, Mary Hamilton
FREEDOM ROAD ENTERPRISE 1980	Fast, Howard Various

FRENCH LIEUTENANT'S WOMAN, THE
UA 1981

Fowles, John
Cape

FROM NOON TILL THREE
UA 1975

Gilroy, Frank D.
N.Y. Doubleday

FULL CIRCLE
CIC 1978

Straub, Peter, *(Julia)*
Cape

G

GAMBLERS, THE
FOX–RANK 1974

Gogol, Nikolai. (P)
Dent

GAME FOR VULTURES
COL–EMI–WAR 1979

Hartmann, Michael
Pan

GEMINI CONTENDERS, THE
ITC 1978

Ludlum, Robert
N.Y. Dell

GETTING OF WISDOM, THE
TEDDERWICK 1979

Richardson, Henry H.
Heinemann

GHOST STORY
UN 1981

Straub, Peter
N.Y. Coward-McCann

GIRL FROM PETROVKA
UN 1975

Feifer, George
Macmillan

GODFATHER PART II, THE
CIC 1974

Puzo, Mario
Heinemann

GODSEND, THE
CANNON 1980

Taylor, Bernard
N.Y. Avon

GOLDEN GATE, THE
ITC 1978

MacLean, Alistair
Collins

GOLDEN GIRL
AVCO EMBASSY 1980

Lear, Peter
Cassell

GOLDEN RENDEZVOUS
RANK 1977

MacLean, Alistair
Collins

GRAY LADY DOWN
CIC 1977

Lavallee, David, *(Event One Thousand)*
Coronet

12

TITLE OF FILM	AUTHOR AND PUBLISHER
GREATEST, THE COL–WAR 1977	Muhamad, Ali Hart-Davis
GREAT EXPECTATIONS SCOTIA-BARBER 1975	Dickens, Charles Various
GREAT SANTINI, THE COL–EMI–WAR 1981	Conroy, Pat N.Y. Avon
GREEN ICE ITC 1981	Browne, Gerald A. N.Y. Delacorte
GULLIVER'S TRAVELS EMI 1976	Swift, Jonathan Various

H

HAND, THE SERENDIPIDY 1981	Brandel, Marc, *(Lizard's Tail, The)* N.Y. Simon & Schuster
HAPPY HOOKER, THE SCOTIA-BARBER 1975	Hollander, Xaviera Talmy-Franklin
HEAD OVER HEELS UA 1979	Beattie, Ann, *(Chilly Scenes of Winter)* N.Y. Popular Library
HEART BEAT COL–EMI–WAR 1980	Cassady, Carolyn Berkeley, Cal.: Creative Arts
HEARTBREAK PASS UA 1975	MacLean, Alistair Collins
HEDDA SCOTIA-BARBER 1977	Ibsen, Henrik, *(Hedda Gabler)*, (P) Various
HELTER SKELTER HEMDALE 1976	Bugliosi, Vincent *and* Gentry, Curt, *(Manson Murders, The)*, Bodley Head
HESTER STREET CONNOISSEUR 1975	Cahen, Abraham, *(Yekl)* Peter Smith
HIDEAWAYS, THE UA 1973	Konigsburg, E.L., *(From the Mixed-up Files of Mr. Basil E. Frankwester)* Macmillan

TITLE OF FILM	AUTHOR AND PUBLISHER

HIDE IN PLAIN SIGHT
CIC 1980

Waller, Leslie
N.Y. Dell

HIDING PLACE, THE
WORLD WIDE FILMS 1974

Boom, Corrie Ten
Hodder & Stoughton

HILL'S ANGELS
DISNEY 1980

Hill, Albert F., *(North Avenue Irregular)*, N.Y. Berkeley

HINDENBURG, THE
CIC 1975

Mooney, Michael M.
Hart-Davis

HITLER: A CAREER
GTO 1978

Fest, Joachim
N.Y. Harcourt

HOMECOMING, THE
SEVEN KEYS 1973

Pinter, Harold. (P)
N.Y. Grove

HOPSCOTCH
RANK 1980

Garfield, Brian
Evans

HOUND OF THE BASKERVILLES, THE
HEMDALE 1978

Doyle, *Sir* Arthur C.
Murray

HOUSE ON GARIBALDI STREET, THE
ITC 1979

Harel, Isser
Deutsch

HOWLING, THE
AVCO EMBASSY 1981

Brandner, Gary
N.Y. Fawcett

HUMAN FACTOR, THE
RANK 1980

Greene, Graham
Heinemann

HUNTER, THE
PAR 1980

Keane, Christopher
N.Y. Arbor House

HURRICANE
ITC 1980

Nordhoff, C.B. *and* Hall, J.N.
Chapman & Hall

I

ICEMAN COMETH, THE
AMERICAN FILM THEATRE 1975

O'Neill, Eugene. (P)
Cape

IN CELEBRATION
SEVEN KEYS 1976

Storey, David. (P)
Cape

TITLE OF FILM	AUTHOR AND PUBLISHER
I NEVER PROMISED YOU A ROSE GARDEN NEW WORLD 1979	Greenberg, Joanne N.Y. New American Library
INNOCENTS WITH DIRTY HANDS FOX—RANK 1975	Neely, Richard Star
IN PRAISE OF OLDER WOMEN COL—EMI—WAR 1978	Vizinczey, Steven Macmillan
INSIDE MOVES BARBER 1981	Walton, Todd N.Y. New American Library
INVASION OF THE BODY SNATCHERS UA 1979	Finney, Jack N.Y. Dell
IPHENIA UA 1978	Euripides. (P) Various
ISLAND, THE CIC 1980	Benchley, Peter N.Y. Doubleday
ISLAND OF DR. MOREAU, THE AMERICAN INTERNATIONAL 1977	Wells, H.G. Heinemann
ISLANDS IN THE STREAM PAR 1977	Hemingway, Ernest Collins
IT SHOULDN'T HAPPEN TO A VET EMI 1976	Herriot, James, *(All Things Bright and Beautiful),* Joseph

J

JORY FOX—RANK 1974	Bass, Milton R. Putnam
JOSEPH ANDREWS UA 1976	Fielding, Henry Various
JULIA FOX 1977	Hellman, Lillian, *(Pentimento)* Macmillan
JUSTINE THE OTHER CINEMA 1976	De Sade, *Marquis* Various

K

KIDNAPPING OF THE PRESIDENT, THE Templeton, Charles
BORDEAUX FILMS 1981   N.Y. Avon

KILLER ELITE, THE   Rostand, Robert
UA 1976   N.Y. Dell

KING OF THE GYPSIES   Maas, Peter
CIC 1980   N.Y. Bantam

KING SOLOMON'S TREASURE   Haggard, *Sir* H. Rider, *(Allan Quater-*
BARBER ROSE 1979   *main),* Various

KNOTS   Laing, R.D.
CINEGATE 1975   N.Y. Random

KRAMER vs KRAMER   Corman, Avery
COL—EMI—WAR 1979   N.Y. New American Library

L

LADY CHATTERLEY'S LOVER   Lawrence, D.H.
COL—EMI—WAR 1981   Heinemann

LADY VANISHES, THE   White, Ethel L., *(Wheel Spins, The)*
RANK 1978   Collins

LAST DETAIL, THE   Ponicsan, Darryl
COL—WAR 1974   Sphere

LAST HARD MAN, THE   Garfield, Brian, *(Gun Down)*
FOX—RANK 1976   N.Y. Dell

LAST TYCOON, THE   Fitzgerald, F. Scott
PAR 1977   Penguin

LATE GREAT PLANET EARTH, THE   Lindsay, Hal *and* Carlson, C.C.
ENTERPRISE 1979   Chicago: Zonderman

LENNY   Barry, Julian (P)
UA 1975   N.Y. Random

LEOPARD IN THE SNOW   Mather, Anne
ANGLO—CANADIAN 1977   Mills & Boon

LETTER FROM AN UNKNOWN WOMAN Zweig, Stefan
UN 1979 Cassell

LITTLE GIRL WHO LIVES DOWN THE Koenig, Laird
LANE, THE Souvenir
RANK 1976

LITTLE LORD FAUNTLEROY Burnett, Frances H.
POLYGRAM 1981 Various

LITTLE PRINCE, THE Saint-Exupery, Antoine
CIC 1974 Various

LITTLE ROMANCE, A Cauvin, Patrick, *(Blind Love)*
COL–EMI–WAR 1979 N.Y. Fawcett

LOGAN'S RUN Nolan, William *and* Johnson, George
MGM 1976 Gollancz

LOOKING FOR MR. GOODBAR Rossner, Judith
CIC 1978 Cape

LORD OF THE RINGS Tolkien, J.R.R., *(Fellowship of the*
UA 1980 *Rings, The : Two Towers, The)*
Allen & Unwin

LOVE BOCCACCIO STYLE Boccaccio, G., *(Decameron, The)*
PRODUCTION ASSOCIATES 1977 Various

LOVIN' MOLLY McMurtry, Larry, *(Leaving Cheyenne)*
GALA 1975 N.Y. Popular Library

LUTHER Osborne, John. (P)
SEVEN KEYS 1973 Faber

M

McVICAR McVicar, John, *(McVicar Himself)*
BRENT WALKER 1980 Hutchinson

MADHOUSE Hall, Angus, *(Devilday-madhouse)*
EMI 1974 Sphere

MAGIC Goldman, William
FOX 1978 N.Y. Dial

MAGICIAN OF LUBLIN, THE
CENTURY CINEMA 1979

Singer, Isaac B.
  Cape

MALEVIL
POLYGRAM 1981

Merle, Robert
  N.Y. Warner

MANDINGO
PAR 1975

Onstott, Kyle
  Pan

MAN IN THE IRON MASK, THE
ITC 1976

Dumas, Alexandre
  Collins

MANITOU, THE
ENTERPRISE 1978

Masterton, Graham
  N.Y. Pinnacle

MAN WHO FELL TO EARTH, THE
BL 1976

Tevis, Walter
  Pan

MAN WHO WOULD BE KING, THE
COL 1976

Kipling, Rudyard
  Macmillan

MARATHON MAN
PAR 1976

Goldman, William
  N.Y. Dial

MARILYN: THE UNTOLD STORY
RANK 1980

Mailer, Norman
  N.Y. Warner

MARTIN
MIRACLE INTERNATIONAL 1979

Romero, George A.
  Futura

MASSACRE IN ROME
GN 1975

Katz, Robert, *(Death in Rome)*
  Cape

MATILDA
RANK 1979

Gallico, Paul
  N.Y. Berkeley

MAYDAY: 40,000 FEET
COL–WAR 1976

Ferguson, Austin, *(Jet Stream)*
  Arrow

MEDUSA TOUCH, THE
ITC 1978

Van Greenaway, Peter
  N.Y. Stein & Day

MEETINGS WITH REMARKABLE MEN
ENTERPRISE 1979

Gurdjieff, G.I.
  N.Y. Dutton

MEMOIRS OF A SURVIVOR
EMI 1981

Leesing, Doris
  Picador

TITLE OF FILM	AUTHOR AND PUBLISHER
MIDNIGHT EXPRESS COL–WAR 1978	Hayes, B. *and* Hoffer, W. N.Y. Dutton
MIDNIGHT MAN, THE UN 1974	Anthony, David, *(Midnight Lady and the Mourning Man, The),* Fontana
MIRROR CRACK'D, THE EMI 1981	Christie, Agatha, *(Mirror Cracked From Side to Side),* Collins
MISTER QUILP EMI 1975	Dickens, Charles, *(Old Curiosity Shop, The),* Various
MOMMIE DEAREST PAR 1981	Crawford, Christiana Hart-Davis
MONSTER CLUB, THE ITC 1981	Chetwynd-Hayes, Ronald Kimber
MOONRAKER UA 1979	Fleming, Ian Cape
MOUSE AND THE WOMAN, THE FACELIFT FILMS 1981	Thomas, Dylan Dent
MY BRILLIANT CAREER GUO 1979	Franklin, Miles N.Y. St. Martin's
MY PLEASURE IS MY BUSINESS MIRACLE FILMS 1975	Hollander, Xaviera, *(Happy Hooker, The),* Talmy-Franklin
MYSTERIES OF THE GODS EMI 1976	Daniken, Erich von, *(Chariots of the Gods),* Corgi

N

NASTY HABITS SCOTIA–BARBER 1977	Spark, Muriel, *(Abbess of Crewe, The)* Penguin
NATIONAL HEALTH COL–WAR 1973	Nichols, Peter. (P) Faber
NEIGHBORS COL–EMI–WAR 1981	Berger, Thomas N.Y. Dell
NIGHTWING COL–EMI–WAR 1980	Smith, M.C. N.Y. Norton

TITLE OF FILM	AUTHOR AND PUBLISHER
NIJINSKY PAR 1980	Nijinsky, Romola N.Y. AMS Press
NIJINSKY PAR 1980	Nijinsky, Vaslor Cal. University of California
NINTH CONFIGURATION, THE ITC 1979	Blatty, William P. N.Y. Bantam
92 IN THE SHADE ITC 1975	McGuane, Thomas N.Y. Farrar
NORTH DALLAS FORTY PAR 1980	Gent, Peter N.Y. Morrow
NORTH SEA HIJACK CIC 1980	Davies, Jack, *(Esther, Ruth and* *Jennifer),* W.H. Allen
NORTH STAR CRUSADE ITC 1978	Katz, William Arrow

O

OH, GOD! COL—WAR 1977	Corman, Avery N.Y. Simon & Schuster
OLIVER'S STORY CIC 1979	Segal, Erich N.Y. Harper
OMEN, THE FOX 1976	Seltzer, David Futura
ONCE IS NOT ENOUGH PAR 1975	Susann, Jacqueline W.H. Allen
ONE FLEW OVER THE CUCKOO'S **NEST** UA 1975	Kesey, Ken N.Y. Viking
ONE OF OUR DINOSAURS IS MISSING DISNEY 1975	Forrest, David, *(Great Dinosaur* *Robbery, The),* Hodder & Stoughton
ON GOLDEN POND CIC 1981	Thompson, Ernest. (P) N.Y. Dodd

TITLE OF FILM	AUTHOR AND PUBLISHER
ONION FIELD, THE AVCO 1979	Wambaugh, Joseph N.Y. Delacorte
ONLY WHEN I LAUGH COL 1981	Simon, Neil, *(Gingerbread Lady)* (P) French
OPERATION DAYBREAK COL–WAR 1975	Burgess, Alan, *(Seven Men at Daybreak)* Mayflower
OPERATION UNDERCOVER UA 1975	Mills, James N.Y. Farrar
ORDINARY PEOPLE PAR 1981	Guest, Judith N.Y. Viking
OSTERMAN WEEKEND, THE AMERICAN COMMUNICATION 1980	Ludlum, Robert N.Y. Dell
OTHERSIDE OF MIDNIGHT, THE FOX 1977	Sheldon, Sidney Hodder & Stoughton
OUTLAW JOSEY WALES, THE COL–WAR 1976	Carter, Forrest, *(Gone to Texas)* N.Y. Delacorte

P

PACK, THE COL–WAR 1977	Fisher, Dave W.H. Allen
PANIC IN NEEDLE PARK FOX–RANK 1971	Mills, James Sphere
PARALLAX VIEW, THE CIC 1974	Singer, Loren N.Y. Doubleday
PASSAGE, THE HEMDALE 1978	Nicolaysen, Bruce, *(Perilous Passge, The)* N.Y. Playboy
PASSENGERS COL–WAR 1976	Dwyer, K.R., *(Shattered)* Barker
PEEPER FOX–RANK 1975	Laumer, Keith, *(Deadfall)* Hale
PEOPLE THAT TIME FORGOT, THE BRENT WALKER 1977	Burroughs, Edgar R. Various

TITLE OF FILM	AUTHOR AND PUBLISHER
PETER PAN DISNEY 1974	Barrie, *Sir* James M. (P) Various
PHYSICAL ASSAULT TITAN 1973	Kolpacoff, Victor, *(Prisoners of Quai Dong, The)*, Sphere
PIECES OF DREAMS UA 1975	Barrett, William E., *(Wine and the Music, The)*, Heinemann
PORTRAIT OF THE ARTIST AS A YOUNG MAN ULYSSES FILM 1977	Joyce, James Cape
POSTMAN ALWAYS RINGS TWICE, THE ITC 1981	Cain, James M. Cape
PRIEST OF LOVE, THE ENTERPRISE 1981	Moore, Harry T. Heinemann
PRINCE AND THE PAUPER, THE FOX 1977	Twain, Mark Various
PRINCE OF THE CITY COL–EMI–WAR 1981	Daley, Robert Hart-Davis
PRISONER OF SECOND AVENUE, THE COL–WAR 1975	Simon, Neil. (P) N.Y. Random
PRISONER OF ZENDA CIC 1979	Hope, Anthony Various
PUMPING IRON CINEGATE 1976	Gaines, Charles *and* Butler, George N.Y. Simon & Schuster
PURSUIT BARBER 1981	Reed, J.D., *(Freefall)* N.Y. Delacorte

Q

QUARTET FOX 1981	Rhys, Jean N.Y. Harper
QUIET DAYS IN CLICHY MIRACLE FILMS 1974	Miller, Henry Calder

R

RAGING BULL
UA 1981

La Motta, J.
N.Y. Bantam

RAGTIME
COL–EMI–WAR 1981

Doctorow, E.L.
Macmillan

RAISE THE TITANIC
ITC 1980

Cussler, Clive
Joseph

RAPE, THE
MIRACLE FILMS 1976

Freeling, Nicholas, *(Because of the Cats)*
Penguin

RED PONY, THE
BL 1976

Steinbeck, John
Various

REINCARNATION OF PETER PROUD, THE
FOX–RANK 1975

Ehrlich, Max
W.H. Allen

REPORT TO THE COMMISSIONER
UA 1975

Mills, James, *(Operation Undercover)*
N.Y. Farrar

RESCUERS
DISNEY 1977

Sharp, Margery, *(Rescuers and Miss Bianca, The)*, N.Y. Dell

RETURN OF THE BIG CAT
DISNEY 1974

Dietz, Lew, *(Year of the Big Cat, The)*
Boston: Little, Brown

RETURN OF THE SOLDIER, THE
BRENT WALKER 1981

West, Rebecca
Virago

RICH AND FAMOUS
MGM 1981

Druten, John van, *(Old Acquaintance)*
(P), French

RICHARD'S THINGS
SOUTHERN PICTURES 1980

Raphael, Frederic
Cape

RIDDLE OF THE SANDS, THE
RANK 1979

Childers, Erskine
Various

RIDE A WILD PONY
DISNEY 1975

Aldridge, James, *(Sporting Proposition, A)*, N.Y. Dell

RITZ, THE
COL–WAR 1976

McNally, Terence. (P)
N.Y. Dodd

ROMANTIC CONGRESSWOMAN, THE
FOX–RANK 1975

Wiseman, Thomas
Cape

ROOSTER COGBURN
UN 1975

Portis, Charles, *(True Grit)*
N.Y. Simon & Schuster

ROSEBUD
UA 1974

Hemingway, Joan *and* Bonnecarrere, P.
N.Y. Morrow

ROSIE DIXON – NIGHT NURSE
COL–WAR 1977

Dixon, Rosie, *(Confessions of a Night Nurse),* Futura

ROUGH CUT
PAR 1980

Lambert, Derek, *(Touch of the Lion's Paw, A),* Corgi

ROYAL FLASH
FOX–RANK 1976

Fraser, G.M.
Barrie & Jenkins

RUSSIAN ROULETTE
FOX–RANK 1975

Ardies, Tom., *(Kosygin is Coming)*
N.Y. Doubleday

S

ST. IVES
COL–WAR 1976

Bleeck, Oliver, *(Procane Chronicle, The)*
N.Y. Morrow

SAILOR'S RETURN, THE
ARIEL 1978

Garnett, David
Chatto & Windus

SAILOR WHO FELL FROM GRACE WITH THE SEA, THE
FOX–RANK 1976

Mishima, Yukio
N.Y. Putnam

SAINT JACK
NEW WORLD 1979

Theroux, Paul
N.Y. Ballantine

SALAMANDER, THE
ITC 1981

West, Morris
N.Y. Morrow

SALON KITTY
FOX 1977

Norden, Peter, *(Madame Kitty)*
Abelard–Schuman

SAME TIME, NEXT YEAR
CIC 1979

Slade, Bernard. (P)
N.Y. Dell

TITLE OF FILM	AUTHOR AND PUBLISHER
SEAWEED CHILDREN, THE PENRITH 1978	Trollope, Anthony, *(Malachi's Cove)* Various
SEA WOLVES, THE RANK 1980	Leasor, James, *(Boarding Party)* Bantam
SEMI-TOUGH UA 1978	Jenkins, Dan N.Y. New American Library
SENTINEL, THE UN 1977	Konvitz, Jeffrey Secker & Warburg
SEVEN ALONE HEMDALE 1974	Morrow, Honore, *(On to Oregon)* N.Y. Morrow
SEVEN-PER-CENT SOLUTION, THE UN 1977	Meyer, Nicholas N.Y. Dutton
SEX SYMBOL, THE WAR 1974	Bessie, Alvah, *(Symbol, The)* Sphere
SHAPE OF THINGS TO COME, THE BARBER DANN 1979	Wells, H.G. Hutchinson
SHINING, THE COL–EMI–WAR 1980	King, Stephen N.Y. New American Library
SHOGUN PAR 1981	Clavell, James N.Y. Dell
SHOOTIST, THE PAR 1976	Swarthout, Glendon N.Y. Doubleday
SHOUT AT THE DEVIL HEMDALE 1976	Smith, Wilbur Heinemann
SIDNEY SHELDON'S BLOODLINE CIC 1979	Sheldon, Sidney, *(Bloodline)* N.Y. Morrow
SILENT PARTNER, THE ENTERPRISE 1978	Bodelsen, Anders Penguin
SILVER BEARS, THE EMI 1978	Erdman, Paul Hutchinson
SLAPSTICK INTERNATIONAL PICTURE 1981	Vonnegut, Kurt N.Y. Delacorte

TITLE OF FILM	AUTHOR AND PUBLISHER
SOMEONE IS KILLING THE GREAT CHEFS OF EUROPE LORIMAR 1978	Lyons, Nan *and* Lyons, Ivan Cape
SOMEWHERE IN TIME CIC 1980	Matheson, Richard, *(Bid Time Return)* Sphere
SORCERER CIC 1978	Arnaud, Georges, *(Wages of Fear, The)* British Publishers Guild
SPACEMAN AND KING ARTHUR, THE DISNEY 1980	Twain, Mark, *(Connecticut Yankee in King Arthur's Court),* Various
SPACE VAMPIRES CANNON 1981	Wilson, Colin N.Y. Random
SPHINX COL–EMI–WAR 1980	Cook, Robin N.Y. Putnam
SPIRAL STAIRCASE, THE COL–WAR 1975	White, Ethel L. Ward Lock
SPY STORY GALA 1976	Deighton, Len Cape
SPY WHO LOVED ME, THE UA 1977	Wood, Christopher Cape
SQUEEZE, THE COL–WAR 1977	Craig, David N.Y. Stein & Day
STAND UP VIRGIN SOLDIERS COL–WAR 1977	Thomas, Leslie Eyre & Methuen
STARTING OVER PAR 1980	Wakefield, Dan N.Y. Dell
STAY HUNGRY UA 1976	Gaines, Charles Chatto & Windus
STEPFORD WIVES, THE CONTEMPORARY 1978	Levin, Ira N.Y. Random
STEPPENWOLF CONTEMPORARY 1976	Hesse, Hermann Various

TITLE OF FILM	AUTHOR AND PUBLISHER
STONE LEOPARD, THE ITC 1978	Forbes, Colin Collins
STORY OF O, THE NEW REALM 1976	Reage, Pauline Olympia Press
STRAIGHT TIME COL–WAR 1978	Bunker, Edward, *(No Beast so Fierce)* N.Y. Dell
STUD, THE BRENT WALKER 1978	Collins, Jackie Mayflower
STUNTMAN, THE FOX 1979	Canutt, Y. *and* Drake, O. N.Y. Walker
SUMMER OF FEAR BRENT WALKER 1978	Duncan, Lois N.Y. Dell
SUNSHINE BOYS, THE CIC–MGM 1975	Simon, Neil. (P) N.Y. Random
SURVIVE STIGWOOD 1976	Blair, C. *jun.* Mayflower
SURVIVOR, THE HEMDALE 1980	Herbert, James N.Y. New American Library
SWARM, THE COL–WAR 1978	Herzog, Arthur Heinemann
SWEET WILLIAM ITC 1980	Bainbridge, Beryl Duckworth
SWISS FAMILY ROBINSON DISNEY 1977	Wyss, J.D. Various
SYBIL BARBER DANN 1979	Schreiber, Flora R. N.Y. Warner

T

TAKE, THE COL–WAR 1974	Newman, G.F., *(Sir, You Bastard)* W.H. Allen

TITLE OF FILM	AUTHOR AND PUBLISHER
TARKA THE OTTER RANK 1978	Williamson, Henry Cape
TELEFON CIC 1978	Wager, W. Barker
TEMPEST, THE MAINLINE 1979	Shakespeare, William. (P) Various
TESS COL 1979	Hardy, Thomas, *(Tess of the D'Urber-villes),* Macmillan
THERE GOES THE BRIDE ENTERPRISE 1981	Cooney, R. *and* Chapman, J. (P) English Theatre Guild
THIEF UA 1981	Hohimer, F., *(Home Invader, The)* Chicago: Chicago Review
THIEVES LIKE US UA 1974	Anderson, Edward N.Y. Avon
3 DAYS OF THE CONDOR PAR 1975	Grady, James, *(Six Days of the Condor)* N.Y. Norton
THIRTY-NINE STEPS, THE RANK 1978	Buchan, John Hodder & Stoughton
TIGERS DON'T CRY RANK 1978	Burmeister, J., *(Running Scared)* Sphere
THIS SWEET SICKNESS ARTIFICIAL EYE 1979	Highsmith, Patricia Heinemann
TIM PISCES 1979	McCullough, C., *(Thorn Birds, The)* N.Y. Harper
TIME AFTER TIME COL–EMI–WAR 1979	Alexander, Karl N.Y. Delacorte
TIN DRUM UA 1979	Grass, Gunter Cape
TOM HORNE COL–EMI–WAR 1980	Horne, Tom University of Oklahoma
TOO MANY CHEFS GTO 1979	Lyons, N. *and* Lyons, I., *(Someone is Killing the Great Chefs of Europe),* Cape

28

TITLE OF FILM	AUTHOR AND PUBLISHER
TO THE DEVIL A DAUGHTER EMI 1976	Wheatley, Dennis Hutchinson
TOUCHED BY LOVE COL 1980	Canada, Lene, *(To Elvis with Love)* N.Y. Everest House
TOWERING INFERNO COL–WAR 1975	Stern, R.M., *(Tower, The)* Pan
TOWERING INFERNO COL–WAR 1975	Scortia, T.M. *and* Robinson, F.M. *(Glass Inferno, The)*, Hodder & Stoughton
TRANS-SIBERIAN EXPRESS ITC 1978	Adler, Warren Macmillan
TREASURE OF MATECUMBRE DISNEY 1976	Taylor, R.L., *(Journey to Matecumbre)* N.Y. New American Library
TRESPASSER, THE COLIN GREGG 1981	Lawrence, D.H. Heinemann
TRUE CONFESSIONS UA 1981	Dunne, John G. Weidenfeld & Nicolson
21 HOURS AT MUNICH ALPHA 1976	Groussard, Serge, *(Blood of Israel, The)* N.Y. Morrow
20,000 LEAGUES UNDER THE SEA DISNEY 1979	Verne, Jules Various
TWILIGHT'S LAST GLEAMING HEMDALE 1977	Wager, Walter, *(Viper Three)* Macmillan
TWO MINUTE WARNING UN 1976	La Fountaine, George N.Y. Coward-McCann

U

UNSUITABLE JOB FOR A WOMAN, AN BOYD 1981	James, P.D. Sphere
URBAN COWBOY CIC 1980	Latham, Aaron N.Y. Bantam

29

TITLE OF FILM	AUTHOR AND PUBLISHER

V

VALENTINO
UA 1977

Steiger, B. *and* Mank, C.
Corgi

VIOLENT STREET
UA 1981

Hohimer, Frank, *(Home Invader, The)*
Chicago: Chicago Review

VOICES
HEMDALE 1973

Lortz, Richard, *(Children of the Night)*
(P), N.Y. Dell

VOYAGE OF THE DAMNED
ITC 1976

Thomas, G. *and* Witts, M.M.
Hodder & Stoughton

W

WAGES OF FEAR
CIC 1978

Arnaud, Georges
British Publishers Guild

WALK WITH LOVE AND DEATH, A
FOX 1969

Koningsberger, Hans
Penguin

WANDERERS, THE
WAR 1980

Price, Richard
N.Y. Avon

WATER BABIES, THE
PRODUCER ASSOCIATES 1979

Kingsley, Charles
Various

WATERSHIP DOWN
CIC 1978

Adams, Richard
Penguin

W.C. FIELDS AND ME
UN 1976

Monti, C. *and* Rice, C.
Joseph

WHEN TIME RAN OUT
COL–EMI–WAR 1980

Thomas, G. *and* Witts, M., *(Day the World Ended, The)*, N.Y. Stein & Day

WHERE'S POPPA?
GEM TOBY 1975

Klane, Robert
Tandem

WHERE THE RED FERN GROWS
EMI 1974

Rawls, Wilson
N.Y. Doubleday

WHITE BUFFALO, THE
EMI 1978

Sale, Richard
N.Y. Simon & Schuster

TITLE OF FILM	AUTHOR AND PUBLISHER
WHITE DAWN, THE CIC 1974	Houston, James Heinemann
WHO'LL STOP THE RAIN? UA 1978	Stone, Robert, *(Dog Soldiers)* Secker & Warburg
WHOSE LIFE IS IT ANYWAY? CIC 1981	Clark, Brian. (P) N.Y. Avon
WHY NOT STAY FOR BREAKFAST? ENTERPRISE 1979	Stone, G. *and* Cooney, R. (P) French
'WHY WOULD I LIE?" MGM 1980	Hodges, H., *(Fabricator, The)* N.Y. Avon
WILD GEESE, THE RANK 1978	Carney, Daniel Heinemann
WINDOW TO THE SKY, A UN 1975	Valens, E.G., *(Long Way Up, A)* N.Y. Harper
WINDWALKER PACIFIC INT. ENTERPRISE 1981	Yorgason, Blaine Salt Lake City: Bookcraft
WINSTANLEY THE OTHER CINEMA 1975	Caute, David, *(Comrade Jacob)* Quartet
WINTER KILLS AVCO EMBASSY 1979	Condon, Richard N.Y. Dial
WISE BLOOD ARTIFICIAL EYE 1979	O'Connor, Flannery N.Y. Farrar
WIZ, THE DISNEY 1979	Baum, Frank, *(Wonderful Wizard of Oz, The)*, Various
WOLFEN, THE WAR 1980	Strieber, Whitley N.Y. Morrow
WORLD IS FULL OF MARRIED MEN, THE NEW REALM 1978	Collins, Jackie W.H. Allen

Y

YOUNG EMMANUELLE
NEW REALM 1977

Arsan, E.
Hart-Davis

YOUR TICKET IS NO LONGER VALID
CAROLCO 1980

Gary, Romain
N.Y. Braziller

AUTHOR INDEX

Author's works which have been filmed are listed under the original title. Film titles which differ from the original are shown in italics.

AUTHOR AND ORIGINAL TITLE	FILM TITLE

A

ADAMS, Richard
WATERSHIP DOWN   CIC 1978
(Penguin)

ADLER, Warren
TRANS-SIBERIAN EXPRESS   ITC 1978
(Macmillan)

ALBEE, Edward
DELICATE BALANCE, A   SEVEN KEYS 1974
(Cape)

ALDRIDGE, James
SPORTING PROPOSITION, A   DISNEY 1975
(N.Y. Dell)   *(Ride a Wild Pony)*

ALEXANDER, Karl
TIME AFTER TIME   COL—EMI—WAR 1979
(N.Y. Delacorte)

AMADO, Jorge
DONA FLOR AND HER TWO   FD 1978
HUSBANDS
(N.Y. Avon)

ANDERSON, Edward
THIEVES LIKE US   UA 1974
(N.Y. Avon)

ANSON, Jay
AMITYVILLE HORROR, THE   AMERICAN INTERNATIONAL
(N.Y. Bantam)   1979

ANTHONY, David
MIDNIGHT LADY AND THE   UN 1974
MOURNING MAN, THE   *(Midnight Man, The)*
(Fontana)

ARDIES, Tom
KOSYGIN IS COMING   FOX—RANK 1975
(N.Y. Doubleday)   *(Russian Roulette)*

ARNAUD, Georges
WAGES OF FEAR, THE — CIC 1978
(British Publishers Guild)
WAGES OF FEAR, THE — CIC 1978
(British Publishers Guild) — *(Sorcerer)* U.S. title

ARSAN, Emmanuelle
EMMANUELLE — SF 1975
(Mayflower)
YOUNG EMMANUELLE — NEW REALM 1977
(Hart-Davis)

ASINOF, E.
TEN SECOND JAILBREAK — COL–WAR 1975
(Joseph) — *(Breakout)*

B

BAINBRIDGE, Beryl
SWEET WILLIAM — ITC 1980
(Duckworth)

BAIRD, Marie-Therese
LESSON IN LOVE, A — BORDEAUX FILMS 1981
(Various) — *(Circle of Two)*

BARAK, Michael
ENIGMA — FILMCREST 1981
(N.Y. New American Library)

BARRETT, William E.
WINE AND THE MUSIC, THE — UA 1975
(Heinemann) — *(Pieces of Dreams)*

BARRIE, *Sir* James M.
PETER PAN (P) — DISNEY 1974
(Various)

BARRY, Julian
LENNY (P) — UA 1975
(N.Y. Random House)

BASS, Milton R.
JORY — FOX–RANK 1972
(Putnam)

36

AUTHOR AND ORIGINAL TITLE	FILM TITLE
BAUM, Frank	
WONDERFUL WIZARD OF OZ, THE	DISNEY 1979
(Various)	*(Wiz, The)*
BEATTIE, Ann	
CHILLY SCENES OF WINTER	UA 1979
(N.Y. Popular Library)	*(Head Over Heels)*
BEHN, Noel	
BIG STICK-UP AT BRINK'S	COL–EMI–WAR 1979
(N.Y. Putnam)	*(Brink's Job, The)*
BENCHLEY, Peter	
DEEP, THE	COL–WAR 1977
(Deutsch)	
ISLAND, THE	CIC 1980
(N.Y. Doubleday)	
BERGER, Thomas	
NEIGHBORS	COL–EMI–WAR 1981
(N.Y. Dell)	
BERNSTEIN, Carl *and* WOODWARD, R.	
ALL THE PRESIDENT'S MEN	COL–WAR 1976
(Secker & Warburg)	
BESSIE, Alvah	
SYMBOL, THE	WAR 1974
(Sphere)	*(Sex Symbol, The)*
BICKHAM, Jack M.	
APPLE DUMPLING GANG, THE	DISNEY 1974
(Hale)	
BLAIR, Clay *jun*	
SURVIVE	STIGWOOD 1976
(N.Y. Macmillan)	
BLATTY, William P.	
NINTH CONFIGURATION, THE	ITC 1979
(N.Y. Bantam)	
BLEECK, Oliver	
PROCANE CHRONICLE, THE	COL–WAR 1976
(N.Y. Morrow)	*(St. Ives)*

AUTHOR AND ORIGINAL TITLE	FILM TITLE

BLYTHE, Ronald
AKINFIELD
(Penguin)

ANGLE FILMS 1975

BOCCACCIO, Giovanni
DECAMERON, THE
(Various)

PRODUCTION ASSOCIATES 1977
(Love Boccaccio Style)

BODELSEN, Anders
SILENT PARTNER, THE
(Penguin)

ENTERPRISE 1978

BOOM, Corrie Ten
HIDING PLACE, THE
(Hodder & Stoughton)

WORLD WIDE FILMS 1974

BRANDEL, Marc
LIZARD'S TAIL, THE
(N.Y. Simon & Schuster)

SERENDIPIDY 1981
(Hand, The)

BRANDNER, Gary
HOWLING, THE
(N.Y. Fawcett)

AVCO EMBASSY 1981

BRASHLER, William
BINGO LONG TRAVELLING ALL-STARS
AND MOTOR KINGS, THE
(N.Y. Harper)

CIC 1976

BRINK, Carol R.
CADDIE WOODLAWN
(Collier-Macmillan)

HEMDALE 1976
(Caddie)

BROWNE, Gerald A.
GREEN ICE
(N.Y. Delacorte)

ITC 1981

BRUCE, J.C.
ESCAPE FROM ALCATRAZ
(N.Y. McGraw)

CIC 1979

BUCHAN, John
THIRTY-NINE STEPS, THE
(Hodder & Stoughton)

RANK 1978

AUTHOR AND ORIGINAL TITLE	FILM TITLE

BUGLIOSI, Vincent *and* GENTRY, C.
MANSON MURDERS, THE   HEMDALE 1976
(Bodley Head)   *(Helter Skelter)*

BUNKER, Edward
NO BEAST SO FIERCE   COL–WAR 1978
(N.Y. Dell)   *(Straight Time)*

BURGESS, Alan
SEVEN MEN AT DAYBREAK   COL–WAR 1975
(Mayflower)   *(Operation Daybreak)*

BURMEISTER, J.
RUNNING SCARED   RANK 1978
(Sphere)   *(Tiger's Don't Cry)*

BURNETT, Frances H.
LITTLE LORD FAUNTLEROY   POLYGRAM 1981
(Various)

BURROUGHS, Edgar R.
AT THE EARTH'S CORE   BL 1976
(N.Y. Ace)
PEOPLE THAT TIME FORGOT, THE   BRENT WALKER 1977
(Various)

C

CAHAN, Abraham
YEKL   CONNOISSEUR 1975
(Peter Smith)   *(Hester Street)*

CAIN, James M.
BUTTERFLY   J & M FILMS 1981
(N.Y. Random House)
POSTMAN ALWAYS RINGS TWICE, THE   ITC 1981
(Cape)

CANADA, Lena
TO ELVIS WITH LOVE   COL 1980
(N.Y. Everest House)   *(Touched by Love)*

CANNING, Victor
RAINBIRD PATTERN, THE   UN 1976
(Heinemann)   *(Family Plot)*

AUTHOR AND ORIGINAL TITLE	FILM TITLE
CANUTT, Yakina *and* **DRAKE, O.** STUNTMAN, THE (N.Y. Walker)	FOX 1979
CARNEY, Daniel WILD GEESE, THE (Heinemann)	RANK 1978
CARROLL, Lewis ALICE IN WONDERLAND (Various)	HEMDALE 1980 *(Alice)*
CARTER, Forrest GONE TO TEXAS (N.Y. Delacorte)	COL–WAR 1976 *(Outlaw Josey Wales, The)*
CASSADY, Carolyn HEART BEAT (Berkeley, Cal: Creative Arts)	COL–EMI–WAR 1980
CAUTE, David COMRADE JACOB (Quartet)	THE OTHER CINEMA 1975 *(Winstanley)*
CAUVIN, Patrick BLIND LOVE (N.Y. Fawcett)	COL–EMI–WAR 1979 *(Little Romance, A)*
CHANDLER, Raymond BIG SLEEP, THE (Hamilton) FAREWELL MY LOVELY (Hamilton)	ITC 1978 FOX–RANK 1975
CHAYEFSKY, Paddy ALTERED STATES (N.Y. Harper)	COL 1981
CHETWYND-HAYES, Ronald MONSTER CLUB, THE (Kimber)	ITC 1981
CHILDERS, Erskine RIDDLE OF THE SANDS, THE (Various)	RANK 1979

AUTHOR AND ORIGINAL TITLE	FILM TITLE
CHOPIN, Kate	
AWAKENING, THE	ENTERPRISE 1981
(N.Y. Avon)	*(End of August, The)*
CHRISTIE, Agatha	
DEATH ON THE NILE	EMI 1978
(Collins)	
EVIL UNDER THE SUN	COL 1981
(Collins)	
MIRROR CRACK'D FROM SIDE TO SIDE	EMI 1981
(Collins)	*(Mirror Crack'd, The)*
TEN LITTLE NIGGERS	COL–EMI–WAR 1979
(Collins) *later published as:*	*(Agatha)*
AND THEN THERE WAS NONE	
CHRISTMAN, Elizabeth	
NICE ITALIAN GIRL, A	BRUT 1978
(N.Y. Dodd)	*(Dangerous Love)*
CLARK, Brian	
WHOSE LIFE IS IT ANYWAY? (P)	CIC 1981
(N.Y. Avon)	
CLAVELL, James	
SHOGUN	PAR 1981
(N.Y. Dell)	
COLLINS, Jackie	
BITCH, THE	BRENT WALKER 1979
(Pan)	
STUD, THE	BRENT WALKER 1978
(Mayflower)	
WORLD IS FULL OF MARRIED MEN,	NEW REALM 1978
THE	
(W.H. Allen)	
COLSON, Charles	
BORN AGAIN	AVCO EMBASSY 1979
(N.Y. Bantam)	
COMPTON, David	
CONTINUOUS KATHERINE MORTEN-	CONTEMPORARY 1979
HOE, THE	*(Death Watch)*
(N.Y. Arrow)	

AUTHOR AND ORIGINAL TITLE	FILM TITLE
CONDON, Richard WINTER KILLS (N.Y. Dial)	AVCO EMBASSY 1979
CONRAD, Joseph DUELLISTS, THE (Fontana)	CIC 1977
CONROY, Pat GREAT SANTINI, THE (N.Y. Avon) WATER IS WIDE, THE (N.Y. Dell)	COL–EMI–FOX 1981 FOX 1976 *(Conrack)*
COOK, Robin COMA (Boston: Little, Brown) SPHINX (N.Y. Putnam)	CIC 1978 COL–EMI–WAR 1980
COONEY, Ray *and* **CHAPMAN, J.** THERE GOES THE BRIDE (P)	ENTERPRISE 1981
CORDER, E.M. DEER HUNTER, THE (Hodder & Stoughton)	COL–EMI 1979
CORMAN, Avery KRAMER vs KRAMER (N.Y. New American Library OH, GOD! (N.Y. Simon & Schuster)	COL–EMI–FOX 1979 COL–WAR 1977
CRAIG, David SQUEEZE, THE (N.Y. Stein & Day)	COL–WAR 1977
CRAWFORD, Christina MOMMIE DEAREST (Hart-Davis)	PAR 1981
CRICHTON, Michael GREAT TRAIN ROBBERY, THE (Cape)	UA 1979 *(First Great Train Robbery, The)*

AUTHOR AND ORIGINAL TITLE	FILM TITLE

CUSSLER, Clive
RAISE THE TITANIC — ITC 1980
(Joseph)

D

DALEY, Robert
PRINCE OF THE CITY — COL–EMI–FOX 1981
(Hart-Davis)

DANIKEN, Erich von
CHARIOTS OF THE GODS — EMI 1976
(Corgi) *(Mysteries of the Gods)*

DAVIES, Jack
ESTHER, RUTH AND JENNIFER — CIC 1980
(W.H. Allen) *(North Sea Hijack)*

DE FELITTA, Frank
AUDREY ROSE — UA 1977
(Collins)

DEIGHTON, Len
SPY STORY — GALA 1976
(Cape)

DE SADE, *Marquis*
JUSTINE — THE OTHER CINEMA 1976
(Various)
JUSTINE — TARGET 1978
(Various) *(Cruel Passion)*

DIAMOND, Paul
CHICKEN CHRONICLES, THE — ALPHA 1980
(N.Y. Dell)

DICKENS, Charles
GREAT EXPECTATIONS — SCOTIA–BARBER 1978
(Various)
OLD CURIOSITY SHOP — EMI 1975
(Various) *(Mister Quilp)*

DIETZ, Lew
YEAR OF THE BIG CAT, THE — DISNEY 1974
(Boston: Little, Brown) *(Return of the Big Cat)*

AUTHOR AND ORIGINAL TITLE	FILM TITLE

DIXON, Rosie
CONFESSIONS OF A NIGHT NURSE
(Futura)

COL—WAR 1977
(Rosie Dixon — Night Nurse)

DOCTOROW, E.L.
RAGTIME
(Macmillan)

COL—EMI—WAR 1981

DOYLE, *Sir* Arthur C.
HOUND OF THE BASKERVILLES, THE
(Murray)

HEMDALE 1978

DRUTEN, John van
OLD ACQUAINTANCE (P)
(French)

MGM 1981
(Rich and Famous)

DUMAS, Alexandre
COUNT OF MONTE CRISTO, THE
(Various)
MAN IN THE IRON MASK, THE
(Various)
MAN IN THE IRON MASK, THE
(Various)
THREE MUSKETEERS
(Various)

SCOTIA—BARBER 1976

ITC 1976

SASCHA WIEN FILMS 1978
(Fifth Musketeer, The)
FOX—RANK 1974
(Four Musketeers, The)

DUNCAN, Lois
SUMMER OF FEAR
(N.Y. Dell)

BRENT WALKER 1978

DUNNE, John G.
TRUE CONFESSIONS
(Weidenfeld & Nicolson)

UA 1981

DWYER, K.R.
SHATTERED
(Barker)

COL—WAR 1976
(Passengers)

E

EHRLICH, Max
REINCARNATION OF PETER PROUD,
THE
(W.H. Allen)

FOX—RANK 1975

44

AUTHOR AND ORIGINAL TITLE	FILM TITLE
ENGLAND, Barry CONDUCT UNBECOMING (P) (French)	BL 1975
ERDMAN, Paul SILVER BEARS, THE (Hutchinson)	EMI 1978
ESZTERHAS, Joe F.I.S.T. (N.Y. Dell)	UA 1978
EURIPIDES IPHENIA (P) (Various)	UA 1978

F

FARLEY, Walter BLACK STALLION (N.Y. Random House)	UA 1979
FAST, Howard FREEDOM ROAD (Various)	ENTERPRISE 1980
FEIFER, George GIRL FROM PETROVKA (Macmillan)	UN 1975
FERGUSON, Austin JET STREAM (Arrow)	COL–WAR 1976 *(Mayday: 40,000 ft.)*
FEST, Joachim HITLER: A CAREER (N.Y. Harcourt)	GTO 1978
FIELDING, Henry JOSEPH ANDREWS (Various) TOM JONES (Various)	UA 1976 CIC 1976 *(Bawdy Adventures of Tom Jones, The)*

AUTHOR AND ORIGINAL TITLE	FILM TITLE

FINNEY, Jack
INVASION OF THE BODY SNATCHERS UA 1974
(N.Y. Dell)

FISHER, Dave
PACK, THE COL–WAR 1977
(W.H. Allen)

FITZGERALD, F. Scott
LAST TYCOON, THE PAR 1977
(Penguin)

FLEMING, Ian
FOR YOUR EYES ONLY UA 1981
(Cape)
MOONRAKER UA 1979
(Cape)

FOLLETT, Kenneth
EYE OF THE NEEDLE, THE UA 1981
(N.Y. New American Library)

FORBES, Colin
AVALANCHE EXPRESS FOX 1979
(N.Y. Dutton)
STONE LEOPARD, THE ITC 1978
(Collins)

FORREST, David
GREAT DINOSAUR ROBBERY, THE DISNEY 1975
(Hodder & Stoughton) *(One of our Dinosaurs is Missing)*

FORSYTH, Frederick
DOGS OF WAR, THE UA 1980
(Hutchinson)

FOWLES, John
FRENCH LIEUTENANT'S WOMAN, THE UA 1981
(Cape)

FRANKLIN, Miles
MY BRILLIANT CAREER GUO 1979
(N.Y. St. Martin's)

46

AUTHOR AND ORIGINAL TITLE	FILM TITLE

FRASER, George M.
ROYAL FLASH — FOX–RANK 1976
(Barrie & Jenkins)

FREELING, Nicholas
BECAUSE OF THE CATS — MIRACLE 1976
(Penguin) *(Rape, The)*

FREEMANTLE, Brian
CHARLIE M — EUSTON 1979
(N.Y. Doubleday) *(Charlie Muggin)*

G

GAINES, Charles
STAY HUNGRY — UA 1976
(Chatto & Windus)

GAINES, Charles *and* BUTLER, G.
PUMPING IRON — CINEGATE 1976
(N.Y. Simon & Schuster)

GAINES, E.J.
AUTOBIOGRAPHY OF MISS JANE — SAGA 1975
PITTMAN, THE
(Bantam)

GALLICO, Paul
BEYOND THE POSEIDON ADVENTURE — COL–EMI–WAR 1979
(Joseph)
MATILDA — RANK 1979
(N.Y. Berkeley)

GANN, Ernest K.
ANTAGONISTS, THE — UA 1980
(N.Y. New American Library) (U.S. title: *Masada*)

GARFIELD, Brian
DEATH SENTENCE — CANNON 1981
(Evans)
DEATH WISH — CIC 1974
(Hodder & Stoughton)
DEATH WISH II — CANNON 1981
(Hodder & Stoughton)

GARFIELD, Brian continued
  GUN DOWN   FOX—RANK 1976
  (N.Y. Dell)   *(Last Hard Man, The)*
  HOPSCOTCH   RANK 1980
  (Evans)

GARFIELD, Leon
  BLACK JACK   ENTERPRISE 1980
  (Longmans)

GARNETT, David
  SAILOR'S RETURN, THE   ARIEL 1978
  (Chatto & Windus)

GARY, Romain
  YOUR TICKET IS NO LONGER VALID   CAROLCO 1980
  (N.Y. Braziller)

GENT, Peter
  NORTH DALLAS FORTY   PAR 1980
  (N.Y. Morrow)

GIFFORD, Thomas
  GLENDOWER LEGACY, THE   FILMPLAN 1980
  (Putnam)   *(Dirty Tricks)*

GILROY, Frank D.
  FROM NOON TILL THREE   UA 1975
  (N.Y. Doubleday)

GOGOL, Nikolai
  GAMBLERS, THE (P)   FOX—RANK 1974
  (Dent) *In:* The Government Inspector
  and other plays

GOLDMAN, William
  MAGIC   FOX 1978
  (N.Y. Dial)
  MARATHON MAN   PAR 1976
  (N.Y. Dial)

GOTTLIEB, Paul
  AGENCY   CAROLCO 1980
  (Sphere)

AUTHOR AND ORIGINAL TITLE	FILM TITLE

GRADY, James
SIX DAYS OF THE CONDOR
(N.Y. Norton)

PAR 1975
(3 Days of the Condor)

GRASS, Gunter
TIN DRUM
(Cape)

UA 1979

GRAY, Simon
BUTLEY (P)
(N.Y. Viking)

SEVEN KEYS 1973

GREENBERG, Joanne
I NEVER PROMISED YOU A ROSE
GARDEN
(N.Y. New American Library)

NEW WORLD 1979

GREENE, Graham
HUMAN FACTOR, THE
(Heinemann)

RANK 1980

GROUSSARD, Serge
BLOOD OF ISRAEL, THE
(N.Y. Morrow)

ALPHA 1976
(21 hours at Munich)

GUEST, Judith
ORDINARY PEOPLE
(N.Y. Viking)

PAR 1981

GURDJIEFF, G.I.
MEETINGS WITH REMARKABLE MEN
(N.Y. Dutton)

ENTERPRISE 1979

GUTHRIE, Woody
BOUND FOR GLORY
(N.Y. Dutton)

UA 1977

H

HAGGARD, *Sir* Rider H.
ALLAN QUATERMAIN
(Various)

BARBER ROSE 1979
(King Solomon's Treasure)

HALL, Angus
    DEVILDAY-MADHOUSE   EMI 1974
    (Sphere)   *(Madhouse)*

HAMMETT, Dashiel
    MALTESE FALCON, THE   COL–WAR 1975
    (Cassell)   *(Black Bird, The)*

HARDY, Thomas
    TESS OF THE D'URBERVILLES   COL 1979
    (Macmillan)   *(Tess)*

HAREL, Isser
    HOUSE ON GARIBALDI STREET, THE   ITC 1979
    (Deutsch)

HARRIS, Thomas
    BLACK SUNDAY   PAR 1977
    (Hodder & Stoughton)

HARTMANN, Michael
    GAME FOR VULTURES   COL–EMI–WAR 1979
    (Pan)

HAYES, Billy *and* HOFFER, W.
    MIDNIGHT EXPRESS   COL–WAR 1978
    (N.Y. Dutton)

HEINRICH, Willi
    WILLING FLESH   EMI 1976
    (Corgi)   *(Cross of Iron)*

HELLMAN, Lillian
    PENTIMENTO   FOX 1977
    (Macmillan)   *(Julia)*

HEMINGWAY, Ernest
    ISLANDS IN THE STREAM   PAR 1977
    (Collins)

HEMINGWAY, Joan *and* BONNECARRERE, P.
    ROSEBUD   UA 1974
    (N.Y. Morrow)

HERBERT, James
  SURVIVOR   HEMDALE 1980
  (N.Y. New American Library)

HERRIOT, James
  ALL THINGS BRIGHT AND BEAUTIFUL   EMI 1976
  (Joseph)   *(It Shouldn't Happen to a Vet)*
  IF ONLY THEY COULD TALK   EMI 1974
  (Joseph)   *(All Creatures Great and Small)*
  IT SHOULDN'T HAPPEN TO A VET   EMI 1974
  (Joseph)   *(All Creatures Great and Small)*

HERZOG, Arthur
  SWARM, THE   COL−WAR 1978
  (Heinemann)

HESSE, Hermann
  STEPPENWOLF   CONTEMPORARY 1976
  (Various)

HIGGINS, Jack
  EAGLE HAS LANDED, THE   ITC 1976
  (Collins)

HIGHSMITH, Patricia
  RIPLEY'S GAME   CINEGATE 1978
  (Hodder & Stoughton)   *(American Friend, The)*
  THIS SWEET SICKNESS   ARTIFICIAL EYE 1979
  (Heinemann)

HILL, Albert
  NORTH AVENUE IRREGULARS   DISNEY 1980
  (N.Y. Berkeley)   *(Hill's Angels)*

HODGES, Hollis
  FABRICATOR, THE   MGM 1980
  (N.Y. Avon)   *("Why Would I Lie?")*

HOHIMER, Frank
  HOME INVADER, THE   UA 1981
  (Chicago: Chicago Review)   *(Violent Street)* U.S. title: *Thief*

HOLLANDER, Xaviera
  HAPPY HOOKER, THE   SCOTIA−BARBER 1975
  (Talmy-Franklin)

AUTHOR AND ORIGINAL TITLE	FILM TITLE

HOLLANDER, Xaviera continued
HAPPY HOOKER, THE   MIRACLE FILMS 1975
(Talmy-Franlin)   *(My Pleasure is my Business)*

HOPE, Anthony
PRISONER OF ZENDA   CIC 1979
(Various)

HORNE, Tom
TOM HORNE   COL−EMI−WAR 1980
(University of Oklahoma Press)

HOUSTON, James
WHITE DAWN, THE   CIC 1974
(Heinemann)

HUDSON, Christopher
FINAL ACT, THE   SAWBUCK 1980
(Joseph)

HUTSON, Sandy
EFF OFF   GALA 1980
(Corgi)   *(Class of Miss MacMichael, The)*

I

IBSEN, Henrik
ENEMY OF THE PEOPLE, AN (P)   ENTERPRISE 1978
(Various)
HEDDA GABLER (P)   SCOTIA−BARBER 1977
(Various)   *(Hedda)*

INNES, Michael
CHRISTMAS AT CANDLESHOE   DISNEY 1977
(Gollancz)   *(Candleshoe)*

J

JACKS, Jeff
MURDER ON THE WILD SIDE   COL−WAR 1973
(N.Y. Fawcett)   *(Black Eye)*

AUTHOR AND ORIGINAL TITLE	FILM TITLE
JAMES, Harrison ABDUCTION (N.Y. Whirlwind)	HEMDALE 1977
JAMES, Henry DAISY MILLER (Hart-Davis) *In:* The Complete Tales, vol. iv.	CIC 1974
JAMES, P.D. UNSUITABLE JOB FOR A WOMAN, AN (Sphere)	BOYD 1981
JENKINS, Dan SEMI-TOUGH (N.Y. New American Library)	UA 1978
JOYCE, James PORTRAIT OF THE ARTIST AS A YOUNG MAN (Cape)	ULYSSES 1977

K

KATZ, Robert DEATH IN ROME (Cape)	GN 1975 *(Massacre in Rome)*
KATZ, William NORTH STAR CRUSADE (Arrow)	ITC 1978
KEANE, Christopher HUNTER, THE (N.Y. Avon)	PAR 1980
KENEALLY, Thomas CHANT OF JIMMIE BLACKSMITH, THE (Angus & Robertson)	FOX 1979
KENNEDY, Adam DOMINO PRINCIPLE, THE (N.Y. Viking)	ITC 1978 *(Domino Killings, The)*

KESEY, Ken
ONE FLEW OVER THE CUCKOO'S NEST UA 1975
(N.Y. Viking)

KEY, Alexander
ESCAPE TO WITCH MOUNTAIN DISNEY 1974
(Various)

KING, Stephen
CARRIE UA 1976
(New English Library)
SHINING, THE COL–EMI–WAR 1980
(N.Y. New American Library)

KINGSLEY, Charles
WATER BABIES, THE PRODUCER ASSOCIATES
(Various) 1979

KIPLING, Rudyard
MAN WHO WOULD BE KING, THE COL 1976
(Macmillan) *In:* Wee Willie Winkie
and other stories

KLANE, Robert
FIRE SALE FOX 1978
(N.Y. Fawcett)
WHERE'S POPPA? GEM TOBY 1975
(Tandem)

KOENIG, Laird
LITTLE GIRL WHO LIVES DOWN THE RANK 1976
LANE, THE
(Souvenir)

KOLPACOFF, Victor
PRISONERS OF QUAI DONG, THE TITAN 1973
(Sphere) *(Physical Assault)*

KONIGSBURG, E.L.
FROM THE MIXED-UP FILES OF UA 1973
MRS. BASIL E. FRANKWESTER *(Hideaways, The)*
(Macmillan)

KONINGSBERGER, Hans
WALK WITH LOVE AND DEATH, A FOX 1969
(Penguin)

AUTHOR AND ORIGINAL TITLE	FILM TITLE
KONVITZ, Jeffrey SENTINEL, THE (Secker & Warburg)	UN 1977
KOONTZ, Dean DEMON SEED (Toronto: Bantam)	MGM 1977
KOSINSKI, Jerzy BEING THERE (N.Y. Bantam)	ITC 1980
KRONBERG, Jeremy EVERY WHICH WAY BUT LOOSE (Hale)	COL—EMI—WAR 1980

L

LA FOUNTAINE, George TWO MINUTE WARNING (N.Y. Coward-McCann)	UN 1976
LAING, R.D. KNOTS (P) (N.Y. Random House)	CINEGATE 1975
LA MOTTA, J. RAGING BULL (N.Y. Bantam)	UA 1981
LAMBERT, Derek TOUCH OF THE LION'S PAW, A (Corgi)	PAR 1980 *(Rough Cut)*
LATHAM, Aaron URBAN COWBOY (N.Y. Bantam)	CIC 1980
LAUMER, Keith DEADFALL (Hale)	FOX—RANK 1975 *(Peeper)*
LAVALLEE, David EVENT 1000 (Coronet)	CIC 1977 *(Gray Lady Down)*

AUTHOR AND ORIGINAL TITLE	FILM TITLE

LAWRENCE, David Herbert
    LADY CHATTERLEY'S LOVER   COL–EMI–FOX 1981
    (Heinemann)
    TRESPASSER, THE   COLIN GREGG 1981
    (Heinemann)

LEA, Timothy
    CONFESSIONS FROM A HOLIDAY CAMP   COL–WAR 1977
    (Sphere)
    CONFESSIONS FROM THE POP SCENE   COL–WAR 1975
    (Futura)   *(Confessions of a Pop Performer)*
    CONFESSIONS OF A DRIVING   COL–WAR 1976
    INSTRUCTOR
    (Sphere)
    CONFESSIONS OF A WINDOW CLEANER   COL–WAR 1974
    (Futura)

LEAR, Robert
    GOLDEN GIRL   AVCO EMBASSY 1980
    (Cassell)

LEASOR, James
    BOARDING PARTY   RANK 1980
    (Bantam)   *(Sea Wolves, The)*

LEESING, Doris
    MEMOIRS OF A SURVIVOR   EMI 1981
    (Picador)

LESLIE, Robert F.
    BEARS AND I, THE   DISNEY 1974
    (N.Y. Ballantine)

LEVIN, Ira
    BOYS FROM BRAZIL, THE   ITC 1978
    (Joseph)
    STEPFORD WIVES, THE   CONTEMPORARY 1978
    (N.Y. Random House)

LEWIS, Oscar
    CHILDREN OF SANCHEZ, THE   HALL BARTLETT 1978
    (N.Y. Random House)

AUTHOR AND ORIGINAL TITLE	FILM TITLE

LINDSAY, Hal *and* CARLSON, C.
LATE GREAT PLANET EARTH, THE — ENTERPRISE 1979
(Chicago: Zonderman)

LORTZ, Richard
CHILDREN OF THE NIGHT (P) — HEMDALE 1973
(N.Y. Dell) — *(Voices)*

LUDLUM, Robert
GEMINI CONTENDERS, THE — ITC 1978
(N.Y. Dell)
OSTERMAN WEEKEND, THE — AMERICAN COMMUNICATION 1980
(N.Y. Dell)

LYNN, Loretta *and* VECSEY, G.
COAL MINER'S DAUGHTER — UN 1980
(Warner)

LYONS, Nan *and* LYONS, I.
SOMEONE IS KILLING THE GREAT — LORIMAR 1978
CHEFS OF EUROPE — *(Too Many Chefs)*
(Cape)

M

McBAIN, Ed
BLOOD RELATIVES — RANK 1978
(Hamilton)

McCULLOUGH, Colleen
THORN BIRDS ,THE — PISCES 1979
(N.Y. Harper) — *(Tim)*

MACDONALD, Ross
DROWNING POOL, THE — COL—WAR 1975
(Fontana)

McGUANE, Thomas
92 IN THE SHADE — ITC 1975
(N.Y. Farrar)

MACLEAN, Alistair
BEAR ISLAND — COL—EMI—WAR 1979
(Collins)

57

MACLEAN, Alistair continued
BREAKHEART PASS   UA 1975
(Collins)   *(Heartbreak Pass)*
FORCE 10 FROM NAVARONE   COL–WAR 1978
(Collins)
GOLDEN GATE, THE   ITC 1978
(Collins)
GOLDEN RENDEZVOUS   RANK 1977
(Collins)

McMURTRY, Larry
LEAVING CHEYENNE   GALA 1975
(N.Y. Popular Library)   *(Lovin' Molly)*

McNALLY, Terrence
RITZ, THE (P)   COL–WAR 1976
(N.Y. Dodd)

McVICAR, John
McVICAR HIMSELF   BRENT WALKER 1980
(Hutchinson)   *(McVicar)*

MAAS, Peter
KING OF THE GYPSIES   CIC 1980
(N.Y. Bantam)

MAETERLINCK, Maurice
BLUE BIRD, THE (P)   FOX 1976
(Methuen)

MAILER, Norman
MARILYN: THE UNTOLD STORY   RANK 1980
(N.Y. Warner)

MALORY, *Sir* Thomas
MORTE D'ARTHUR, LE   COL–EMI–WAR 1981
(Various)   *(Excalibur)*

MANNIX, Daniel
FOX AND THE HOUND   DISNEY 1981
(Various)

MARASCO, Robert
BURNT OFFERINGS   UA 1976
(Coronet)

AUTHOR AND ORIGINAL TITLE	FILM TITLE
MARLOWE, Derek	
ECHOES OF CELANDINE	CINEGATE 1977
(Penguin)	*(Disappearance, The)*
MASON, A.E.W.	
FOUR FEATHERS, THE	TRIDENT BARBER 1978
(Hodder & Stoughton)	
MASTERTON, Graham	
MANITOU, THE	ENTERPRISE 1978
(N.Y. Pinnacle)	
MATHER, Anne	
LEOPARD IN THE SNOW	ANGLO-CANADIAN 1977
(Mills & Boon)	
MATHESON, Richard	
BID TIME RETURN	CIC 1980
(Sphere)	*(Somewhere in Time)*
MERLE, Robert	
MALEVIL	POLYGRAM 1981
(N.Y. Warner)	
MEYER, Nicholas	
SEVEN-PER-CENT SOLUTION, THE	UN 1977
(N.Y. Dutton)	
MICHENER, James A.	
CARAVANS	BORDEAUX FILMS 1979
(N.Y. Random House)	
MILLER, Henry	
QUIET DAYS IN CLICHY	MIRACLE FILMS 1974
(Calder)	
MILLS, James	
PANIC IN NEEDLE PARK	FOX—RANK 1971
(Sphere)	
REPORT TO THE COMMISSIONER	UN 1975
(N.Y. Farrar)	*(Operation Undercover)* U.S. title
MISHIMA, Yukio	
SAILOR WHO FELL FROM GRACE WITH THE SEA, THE	FOX—RANK 1976
(N.Y. Putnam)	

AUTHOR AND ORIGINAL TITLE	FILM TITLE
MONTI, Carlotta *and* **RICE, C.** W.C. FIELDS AND ME (Joseph)	UN 1976
MOONEY, Michael M. HINDENBURG, THE (Hart-Davis)	CIC 1975
MOORE, Harry T. PRIEST OF LOVE, THE (Heinemann)	ENTERPRISE 1981
MOORE, Robin DUBAI (N.Y. Doubleday)	AMERICAN COMMUNICATION 1980
MORROW, Honore ON TO OREGON (N.Y. Morrow)	HEMDALE 1974 *(Seven Alone)*
MUHAMAD, Ali GREATEST, THE (Hart-Davis)	COL–WAR 1977

N

NABOKOV, Vladimir DESPAIR (N.Y. Putnam)	GALA 1978
NEELY, Richard INNOCENTS WITH DIRTY HANDS (Star)	FOX–RANK 1975
NEWMAN, G.F. SIR, YOU BASTARD (W.H. Allen)	COL–WAR 1974 *(Take, The)*
NICHOLS, Peter NATIONAL HEALTH, THE (P) (Faber)	COL–WAR 1973
NICOLAYSEN, Bruce PERILOUS PASSAGE, THE (N.Y. Playboy)	HEMDALE 1978 *(Passage, The)*

AUTHOR AND ORIGINAL TITLE	FILM TITLE
NIJINSKY, Romola NIJINSKY (N.Y. AMS Press)	PAR 1980
NIJINSKY, Vaslov NIJINSKY (University of California)	PAR 1980
NOLAN, Frederick ALGONQUIN PROJECT, THE (N.Y. Morrow)	MGM 1978
NOLAN, William F. *and* **JOHNSON, G.** LOGAN'S RUN (Gollancz)	MGM 1976
NORDEN, Peter MADAME KITTY (Abelard-Schuman)	FOX 1977 *(Salon Kitty)*
NORDHOFF, Charles *and* **HALL, J.** HURRICANE (Chapman & Hall)	ITC 1980

O

O'CONNOR, Flannery WISE BLOOD (N.Y. Farrar)	ARTIFICIAL EYE 1979
O'NEILL, Eugene ICEMAN COMETH, THE (P) (Cape)	AMERICAN FILM THEATRE 1975
ONSTOTT, Kyle DRUM (Pan) MANDINGO (Pan)	PAR 1976 PAR 1975
OSBORNE, John ENTERTAINER, THE (P) (Evans) LUTHER (P) (Faber)	SEVEN KEYS 1975 SEVEN KEYS 1973

P

PAGE, Thomas
HEPHAESTUS PLAGUE, THE   PAR 1975
(Putnam)   *(Bug)*

PERTWEE, Michael
DON'T JUST LIE THERE, SAY   RANK 1975
SOMETHING (P)
(French)

PINTER, Harold
HOME COMING, THE (P)   SEVEN KEYS 1973
(N.Y. Grove)

PLATH, Sylvia
BELL JAR, THE   AVCO EMBASSY 1978
(N.Y. Harper)

PONICSAN, Darryl
LAST DETAIL, THE   COL–WAR 1974
(Sphere)

PORTIS, Charles
TRUE GRIT   UN 1975
(N.Y. Simon & Schuster)   *(Rooster Cogburn)*

POWERS, Art *and* MISENHEIMER, M.
FRAMED   CIC 1974
(Pinnacle)

PRICE, Richard
BLOODBROTHERS   COL–WAR 1978
(N.Y. Bantam)
WANDERERS, THE   WAR 1980
(N.Y. Avon)

PUZO, Mario
GODFATHER, THE   CIC 1974
(Heinemann)   *(Godfather Part II, The)*

R

RAE, John
CUSTARD BOYS, THE   FOREST HALL 1980
(N.Y. Random House

RANDALL, Bob
FAN, THE   CIC 1981
(N.Y. Random House)

RAWLS, Wilson
WHERE THE RED FERN GROWS   EMI 1974
(N.Y. Doubleday)

RAPHAEL, Frederic
RICHARD'S THINGS   SOUTHERN 1980
(Cape)

REAGE, Pauline
STORY OF O, THE   NEW REALM 1976
(Olympia)

REED, J.D.
FREEFALL   BARBER 1981
(N.Y. Delacorte)   *(Pursuit)*

REMARQUE, Erich M.
ALL QUIET ON THE WESTERN FRONT   ITC 1980
(Putnam)
HEAVEN HAS NO FAVOURITES   COL—WAR 1977
(N.Y. Harcourt)   *(Bobby Deerfield)*

RHYS, Jean
QUARTET   FOX 1981
(N.Y. Harper)

RICHARDSON, H.H.
GETTING OF WISDOM, THE   TEDDERWICK 1979
(Heinemann)

RICHLER, Mordecai
APPRENTICESHIP OF DUDDY   RANK 1975
KRAVITZ, THE
(Deutsch)

AUTHOR AND ORIGINAL TITLE	FILM TITLE
ROBBINS, Harold BETSY, THE (New English Library)	UA 1978
ROBESON, Kenneth DOC SAVAGE – THE MAN OF BRONZE (Corgi)	COL–WAR 1975
RODGERS, Mary FREAKY FRIDAY (Hamilton)	DISNEY 1976
ROMERO, George A. MARTIN (Futura)	MIRACLE INTERNATIONAL 1979
ROSSNER, Judith LOOKING FOR MR. GOODBAR (Cape)	CIC 1978
ROSTAND, Robert KILLER ELITE, THE (N.Y. Dell)	UA 1976
RYAN, Cornelius BRIDGE TOO FAR, A (Hamilton)	UA 1977

S

SAINT-EXUPERY, Antoine LITTLE PRINCE, THE (Various)	CIC 1974
SALE, Richard WHITE BUFFALO, THE (N.Y. Simon & Schuster)	EMI 1978
SANDERS, Lawrence FIRST DEADLY SIN, THE (Star)	CIC 1981
SCHREIBER, Flora R. SYBIL (N.Y. Warner)	BARBER–DANN 1979

SCORTIA, T. *and* **ROBINSON, F.**
GLASS INFERNO, THE
(Hodder & Stoughton)

COL—WAR 1975
(Towering Inferno, The)

SEGAL, Erich
OLIVER'S STORY
(N.Y. Harper)

CIC 1979

SELTZER, David
OMEN, THE
(Futura)

FOX 1976

SEYMOUR, Henry
INFERNAL IDOL
(N.Y. Avon)

EMI 1974
(Craze)

SHAFFER, Peter
EQUUS
(Deutsch)

UA 1977

SHAGAN, Steve
FORMULA, THE
(N.Y. Bantam)

MGM 1980

SHAKESPEARE, William
TEMPEST, THE (P)
(Various)

MAINLINE 1979

SHARP, Margery
RESCUERS AND MISS BIANCA, THE
(N.Y. Dell)

DISNEY 1977
(Rescuers)

SHELDON, Sidney
BLOODLINE
(N.Y. Morrow)
OTHER SIDE OF MIDNIGHT, THE
(Hodder & Stoughton)

CIC 1979
(Sidney Sheldon's Bloodline)
FOX 1977

SHERRIFF, R.C.
JOURNEYS END
(Gollancz)

EMI 1976
(Aces High)

SIMON, Neil
CALIFORNIA SUITE (P)
(N.Y. Random House)

COL 1979

AUTHOR AND ORIGINAL TITLE	FILM TITLE
SIMON, Neil continued	
CHAPTER TWO (P)	COL–EMI–WAR 1980
(N.Y. Random House)	
GINGERBREAD LADY (P)	COL 1981
(French)	*(Only When I Laugh)*
PRISONER OF SECOND AVENUE (P)	COL–WAR 1975
(N.Y. Random House)	
SUNSHINE BOYS, THE (P)	CIC–MGM 1975
(N.Y. Random House)	
SIMON, Roger L.	
BIG FIX, THE	CIC 1979
(N.Y. Pocket Books)	
SINGER, Isaac B.	
MAGICIAN OF LUBLIN, THE	CENTURY CINEMA 1979
(Cape)	
SINGER, Loren	
PARALLAX VIEW, THE	CIC 1974
(N.Y. Doubleday)	
SLADE, Bernard	
SAME TIME, NEXT YEAR (P)	CIC 1979
(N.Y. Dell)	
SMITH, Martin C.	
NIGHTWING	COL–EMI–WAR 1980
(N.Y. Norton)	
SMITH, Wilbur	
SHOUT AT THE DEVIL	HEMDALE 1976
(Heinemann)	
SPARK, Muriel	
ABBESS OF CREWE, THE	SCOTIA–BARBER 1976
(N.Y. Viking)	*(Abbess, The) also: (Nasty Habits)*
SPENCER, Scott	
ENDLESS LOVE	BARBER 1981
(N.Y. Knopf)	
STACPOOLE, H. de V.	
BLUE LAGOON, THE	COL 1980
(Various)	

STANTON, Will
GOLDEN EVENINGS OF SUMMER, THE — DISNEY 1974
(N.Y. Lancer) — *(Charley and the Angel)*

STEIGER, B. *and* **MANE, C.**
VALENTINO — UA 1977
(Corgi)

STEINBECK, John
CANNERY ROW — MGM 1981
(Heinemann)
RED PONY, THE — BL 1976
(Various)

STERN, Richard M.
TOWER, THE — COL–WAR 1975
(Pan) — *(Towering Inferno, The)*

STOKER, Bram
DRACULA — CIC 1979
(Various) — KODIAK FILMS 1979
— *(Dracula Sucks)*
JEWEL OF THE SEVEN STARS — COL–EMI–WAR 1980
(Jarrolds) — *(Awakening, The)*

STONE, Gene *and* **COONEY, R.**
WHY NOT STAY FOR BREAKFAST (P) — ENTERPRISE 1979
(French)

STONE, Robert
DOG SOLDIERS — UA 1978
(Secker & Warburg) — (U.S. title: *Who'll Stop the Rain?*)

STOREY, David
IN CELEBRATION (P) — SEVEN KEYS 1976
(Cape)

STRAUB, Peter
FULL CIRCLE — CIC 1978
(Cape) — *(Julia)*
GHOST STORY — UN 1981
(N.Y. Coward–McCann)

STRIEBER, Whitley
WOLFEN, THE — COL–EMI–WAR 1980
(N.Y. Morrow)

SUSANN, Jacqueline
ONCE IS NOT ENOUGH   PAR 1975
(W.H. Allen)

SWARTHOUT, Glendon
SHOOTIST, THE   PAR 1976
(N.Y. Doubleday)

SWIFT, Jonathan
GULLIVER'S TRAVELS   EMI 1976
(Various)

T

TAYLOR, Bernard
GODSEND, THE   CANNON 1980
(N.Y. Avon)

TAYLOR, Robert
JOURNEY TO MATECUMBE   DISNEY 1976
(N.Y. New American Library)   *(Treasure of Matecumbe)*

TEMPLETON, Charles
KIDNAPPING OF THE PRESIDENT, THE BORDEAUX FILMS 1981
(N.Y. Avon)

TEVIS, Walter
MAN WHO FELL TO EARTH, THE BL 1976
(Pan)

THEROUX, Paul
SAINT JACK   NEW WORLD 1979
(N.Y. Ballentine)

THIELE, Colin
BLUE FIN   SOUTH AUSTRALIA FILMS
(Collins)   1978

THOMAS, Dylan
MOUSE AND THE WOMAN, THE FACELIFT FILMS 1981
(In: Short Stories of ...)
(Dent)

AUTHOR AND ORIGINAL TITLE	FILM TITLE
THOMAS, Gordon *and* **Witts, M.**	
DAY THE WORLD ENDED, THE	COL—EMI—WAR 1980
(N.Y. Stein & Day)	*(When Time Ran Out)*
VOYAGE OF THE DAMNED	ITC 1976
(Hodder & Stoughton)	
THOMAS, Leslie	
DANGEROUS DAVIES – THE LAST	INNER CIRCLE 1980
DETECTIVE	
(Eyre & Methuen)	
STAND UP VIRGIN SOLDIERS	COL—WAR 1977
(Eyre & Methuen)	
THOMPSON, Ernest	
ON GOLDEN POND	CIC 1981
(N.Y. Dodd)	
THORNBURG, Newton	
CUTTER AND BONE	UA 1981
(Heinemann)	*(Cutter's Way)*
THYNNE, Alexander	
BLUE BLOOD	NATIONWIDE 1974
(Sphere)	
TOLKIEN, J.R.R.	
FELLOWSHIP OF THE RINGS, THE	UA 1980
TWO TOWERS, THE	*(Lord of the Rings)*
(Allen & Unwin)	
TREVANIAN	
EIGER SANCTION, THE	CIC 1975
(Heinemann)	
TROLLOPE, Anthony	
MALACHI'S COVE	PENRITH 1978
(Various)	*(Seaweed Children, The)*
TRYON, Thomas	
CROWNED HEADS	MAINLINE 1979
(N.Y. Fawcett)	*(Fedora)*
TWAIN, Mark	
CONNECTICUT YANKEE IN KING	DISNEY 1980
ARTHUR'S COURT	*(Spaceman and King Arthur, The)*
(Various)	

TWAIN, Mark continued
PRINCE AND THE PAUPER, THE
(Various)

FOX 1977
(U.S. title: *Crossed Swords*)

V

VALENS, E.G.
LONG WAY UP, A
(N.Y. Harper)

UN 1975
(Window to the Sky, A)

VAN GREENAWAY, Peter
MEDUSA TOUCH, THE
(N.Y. Stein & Day)

ITC 1978

VASQUEZ-FIGUEROA, Alberto
EBANO
(Hale)

COL–EMI 1979
(Ashanti)

VERNE, Jules
20,000 LEAGUES UNDER THE SEA
(Various)

DISNEY 1979

VIZINCZEY, Steven
IN PRAISE OF OLDER WOMEN
(Macmillan)

COL–EMI–WAR 1978

VONNEGUT, Kurt
SLAPSTICK
(N.Y. Delacorte)

INTERNATIONAL PICTURE
SHOW 1981

W

WAGER, Walter
TELEFON
(Barker)
VIPER THREE
(Macmillan)

CIC 1978

HEMDALE 1977
(Twilight's Last Gleaming)

WAKEFIELD, Dan
STARTING OVER
(N.Y. Dell)

PAR 1980

AUTHOR AND ORIGINAL TITLE	FILM TITLE
WALKER, Gerald CROKING (W.H. Allen)	ITC 1980
WALLER, Leslie HIDE IN PLAIN SIGHT (N.Y. Dell)	CIC 1980
WALTON, Todd INSIDE MOVES (N.Y. New American Library)	BARBER 1981
WAMBAUGH, Joseph BLACK MARBLE, THE (N.Y. Dell) BLUE NIGHT (Joseph) CHOIR BOYS, THE (Weidenfeld & Nicolson) ONION FIELD, THE (N.Y. Delacorte)	AVCO 1980 BUTCHER 1973 GTO 1977 AVCO 1979
WARD, Robert CATTLE ANNIE AND LITTLE BRITCHES (N.Y. Ace)	HEMDALE 1980
WELLS, H.G. ISLAND OF Dr. MOREAU, THE (Heinemann) SHAPE OF THINGS TO COME, THE (Hutchinson) VALLEY OF THE ANTS, THE (Fontana)	AMERICAN INTERNATIONAL 1977 BARBER DANN 1979 BRENT WALKER 1978 *(Empire of the Ants)*
WEST, Morris DEVIL'S ADVOCATE, THE (Heinemann) SALAMANDER, THE (N.Y. Morrow)	RANK 1977 ITC 1981
WEST, Nathaniel DAY OF THE LOCUST, THE (N.Y. New Directions)	CIC 1975

71

AUTHOR AND ORIGINAL TITLE	FILM TITLE
WEST, Rebecca RETURN OF THE SOLDIER (Virago)	BRENT WALKER 1981
WHEATLEY, Dennis TO THE DEVIL A DAUGHTER (Hutchinson)	EMI 1976
WHITE, Ethel L. SPIRAL STAIRCASE, THE (Ward Lock) WHEEL SPINS, THE (Collins)	COL–WAR 1975 RANK 1979 *(Lady Vanishes, The)*
WILLARD, John CAT AND THE CANARY, THE (P) (Hudson)	GALA 1981
WILLEFORD, Charles COCKFIGHTER (N.Y. Crown)	EMI 1974
WILLIAMSON, Henry TARKA THE OTTER (Cape)	RANK 1978
WILSON, Colin SPACE VAMPIRES (N.Y. Random House)	CANNON 1981
WISEMAN, Thomas ROMANTIC CONGRESSWOMAN, THE (Cape)	FOX–RANK 1975
WOLFF, Ruth ABDICATION, THE (P) (Paperback Library)	COL–WAR 1974
WOLLASTON, Nicholas ECLIPSE (Macmillan)	GALA 1976
WOOD, Christopher SPY WHO LOVED ME, THE (Cape)	UA 1977

AUTHOR AND ORIGINAL TITLE	FILM TITLE

WYSS, Johann D.
SWISS FAMILY ROBINSON   DISNEY 1977
(Various)

Y

YALLOP, David
BEYOND REASONABLE DOUBT   J & M FILMS 1980
(Hodder & Stoughton)

YORGASON, Blaine
WINDWALKER   PACIFIC INTERNATIONAL
(Salt Lake City: Bookcraft)   1981

Z

ZELAZNY, Roger
DAMNATION ALLEY   FOX 1978
(N.Y. Putnam)

ZWEIG, Stefan
LETTER FROM AN UNKNOWN WOMAN   UN 1979
(Cassell)

CHANGE OF ORIGINAL TITLE INDEX

Film companies frequently change the original title of the book or play on screening. This alphabetical index gives the author's original and published title of his work, followed by the screen title where the two differ.

ORIGINAL TITLE	FILM TITLE
ABBESS OF CREWE, THE Spark, M.	**ABBESS, THE** SCOTIA–BARBER 1976 **NASTY HABITS** SCOTIA–BARBER 1977
ALICE IN WONDERLAND Carroll, L.	**ALICE** HEMDALE 1980
ALGONQUIN PROJECT, THE Nolan, F.	**BRASS TARGET** MGM 1978
ALLAN QUATERMAIN Haggard, *Sir* H.R.	**KING SOLOMON'S TREASURE** BARBER ROSE 1979
ALL THINGS BRIGHT AND BEAUTIFUL Herriot, J.	**IT SHOULDN'T HAPPEN TO A VET** EMI 1976
AND THEN THERE WERE NONE Christie, A. *(Originally published as: Ten Little Niggers)*	**AGATHA** COL–EMI–WAR 1979
AWAKENING, THE Chopin, K.	**END OF AUGUST, THE** ENTERPRISE 1981
BECAUSE OF THE CATS Freeling, N.	**RAPE, THE** MIRACLE FILMS 1976
BID TIME RETURN Matheson, R.	**SOMEWHERE IN TIME** CIC 1980
BIG STICK-UP AT BRINK'S Behn, N.	**BRINK'S JOB, THE** COL–EMI–WAR 1979
BLIND LOVE Cauvin, P.	**LITTLE ROMANCE, A** COL–EMI–WAR 1979
BLOOD OF ISRAEL, THE Groussard, S.	**21 HOURS AT MUNICH** ALPHA 1976
BOARDING PARTY Leasor, J.	**SEA WOLVES, THE** RANK 1980
CADDIE WOODLAWN Brink, C.R.	**CADDIE** HEMDALE 1976

CHARIOT OF THE GODS Daniken, E.	**MYSTERIES OF THE GODS** EMI 1976
CHARLIE M Freemantle, B.	**CHARLIE MUGGIN** EUSTON FILMS 1979
CHILDREN OF THE NIGHT (P) Lortz, R.	**VOICES** HEMDALE 1973
CHILLY SCENES OF WINTER Beattie, A.	**HEAD OVER HEELS** UA 1979
CHRISTMAS AT CANDLESHOE Innes, M.	**CANDLESHOE** DISNEY 1977
COMRADE JACOB Caute, D.	**WINSTANLEY** THE OTHER CINEMA 1975
CONFESSIONS FROM THE POP SCENE Lea, T.	**CONFESSIONS OF A POP PERFORMER** COL–WAR 1975
CONFESSIONS OF A NIGHT NURSE Dixon, R.	**ROSIE DIXON – NIGHT NURSE** COL–WAR 1977
CONNECTICUT YANKEE IN KING ARTHUR'S COURT Twain, M.	**SPACEMAN AND KING ARTHUR, THE** DISNEY 1980
CONTINUOUS KATHERINE MORTENHOE, THE Compton, D.	**DEATH WATCH** CONTEMPORARY 1979
CROWNED HEADS Tryon, T.	**FEDORA** MAINLINE 1979
CUTTER AND BONE Thornburg, N.	**CUTTER'S WAY** UA 1981
DAY THE WORLD ENDED, THE Thomas, G. & Witts, M.	**WHEN TIME RAN OUT** COL–EMI–WAR 1980
DEADFALL Laumer, K.	**PEEPER** FOX–RANK 1975
DEATH IN ROME Katz, R.	**MASSACRE IN ROME** GN 1975

ORIGINAL TITLE	FILM TITLE
DECAMERON, THE Boccaccio, G.	**LOVE BOCCACCIO STYLE** PRODUCTION ASSOCIATES 1977
DEVILDAY-MADHOUSE Hall, A.	**MADHOUSE** EMI 1974
DOMINO PRINCIPLE, THE Kennedy, A.	**DOMINO KILLINGS, THE** ITC 1978
DRACULA Stoker, B.	**DRACULA SUCKS** KODIAK 1979
EBANO Vasquez-Figueroa, A.	**ASHANTI** COL–EMI 1979
ECHOES OF CELANDINE Marlowe, D.	**DISAPPEARANCE, THE** CINEGATE 1977
EFF OFF Hutson, S.	**CLASS OF MISS MacMICHAEL, THE** GALA 1980
ESTHER, RUTH AND JENNIFER Davies, J.	**NORTH SEA HIJACK** CIC 1980
EVENT 1000 Lavallee, D.	**GRAY LADY DOWN** CIC 1977
FABRICATOR, THE Hodges, H.	**"WHY SHOULD I LIE?"** MGM 1980
FELLOWSHIP OF THE RING, THE Tolkien, J.R.R.	**LORD OF THE RINGS** UA 1980
FREEFALL Reed, J.D.	**PURSUIT** BARBER 1981
FROM THE MIXED-UP TALES OF MR. BASIL E. FRANKWESTER Konigsburg, E.L.	**HIDEAWAYS, THE** UA 1973
GINGERBREAD LADY (P) Simon, N.	**ONLY WHEN I LAUGH** COL 1981
GLASS INFERNO, THE Scortia, T. & Robinson, F.	**TOWERING INFERNO, THE** COL–WAR 1975

ORIGINAL TITLE	FILM TITLE
GLENDOWER LEGACY, THE Gifford, T.	**DIRTY TRICKS** FILMPLAN 1980
GODFATHER, THE Puzo, M.	**GODFATHER PART II, THE** CIC 1974
GOLDEN EVENINGS OF SUMMER, THE Stanton, W.	**CHARLEY AND THE ANGEL** DISNEY 1974
GONE TO TEXAS Carter, F.	**OUTLAW JOSEY WALES, THE** COL–WAR 1976
GREAT DINOSAUR ROBBERY, THE Forrest, D.	**ONE OF OUR DINOSAURS IS MISSING** DISNEY 1975
GREAT TRAIN ROBBERY, THE Crichton, M.	**FIRST GREAT TRAIN ROBBERY, THE** UA 1979
GUN DOWN Garfield, B.	**LAST HARD MAN, THE** FOX–RANK 1976
HAPPY HOOKER, THE Hollander, X.	**MY PLEASURE IS MY BUSINESS** MIRACLE FILMS 1975
HEAVEN HAS NO FAVOURITES Remarque, E.M.	**BOBBY DEERFIELD** COL–WAR 1977
HEDDA GABLER (P) Ibsen, H.	**HEDDA** SCOTIA–BARBER 1977
HEPHAESTUS PLAGUE, THE Page, T.	**BUG** PAR 1975
HOME INVADER Hohimer, F.	**VIOLENT STREET** UA 1981 *(U.S. Title: Thief)*
IF ONLY THEY COULD TALK Herriot, J.	**ALL CREATURES GREAT AND SMALL** EMI 1974
IT SHOULDN'T HAPPEN TO A VET Herriot, J.	**ALL CREATURES GREAT AND SMALL** EMI 1974

ORIGINAL TITLE	FILM TITLE
JET STREAM Ferguson, A.	**MAYDAY: 40,000 FT.** COL–WAR 1976
JEWEL OF THE SEVEN STARS Stoker, B.	**AWAKENING, THE** COL–EMI–WAR 1980
JOURNEY TO MATECUMBE Taylor, R.L.	**TREASURE OF MATECUMBE** DISNEY 1976
JULIA Straub, P.	**FULL CIRCLE** CIC 1978
JUSTINE De Sade, *Marquis*	**CRUEL PASSION** TARGET 1978
KOSYGIN IS COMING Ardies, T.	**RUSSIAN ROULETTE** FOX–RANK 1975
LEAVING CHEYENNE McMurtry, L.	**MOVIN' MOLLY** GALA 1975
LESSON IN LOVE, A Baird, M-T.	**CIRCLE OF TWO** BORDEAUX FILMS 1981
LIZARD'S TAIL, THE Brandel, M.	**HAND, THE** SERENDIPIDY 1981
LONG WAY UP, A Valens, E.G.	**WINDOW TO THE SKY, A** UN 1975
McVICAR BY HIMSELF McVicar, J.	**McVICAR** BRENT WALKER 1980
MADAM KITTY Norden, P.	**SALON KITTY** FOX 1977
MALACHI'S COVE Trollope, A.	**SEAWEED CHILDREN, THE** PENRITH 1978
MALTESE FALCON, THE Hammett, D.	**BLACK BIRD, THE** COL–WAR 1975
MAN IN THE IRON MASK, THE Dumas, A.	**FIFTH MUSKETEER, THE** SASCHA WIEN FILMS 1978
MANSON MURDERS, THE Bugliosi, V. & Gentry, C.	**HELTER SKELTER** HEMDALE 1976

ORIGINAL TITLE	FILM TITLE
MIDNIGHT LADY AND THE MOURNING MAN, THE Anthony, D.	**MIDNIGHT MAN, THE** UN 1974
MIRROR CRACK'D FROM SIDE TO SIDE, THE Christie, A.	**MIRROR CRACK'D, THE** EMI 1981
MORTE D'ARTHUR, LE Malory, *Sir* T.	**EXCALIBUR** COL—EMI—WAR 1981
MURDER ON THE WILD SIDE Jacks, J.	**BLACK EYE** COL—WAR 1973
NICE ITALIAN GIRL, A Christman, E.	**DANGEROUS LOVE** BRUT 1978
NO BEAST SO FIERCE Bunker, E.	**STRAIGHT TIME** COL—WAR 1978
NORTH AVENUE IRREGULARS Hill, A.F.	**HILL'S ANGELS** DISNEY 1980
OLD ACQUAINTANCE (P) Druten, J. van	**RICH AND FAMOUS** MGM 1981
OLD CURIOSITY SHOP Dickens, C.	**MISTER QUILP** EMI 1975
ON TO OREGON Morrow, H.	**SEVEN ALONE** HEMDALE 1974
PENTIMENTO Hellman, L.	**JULIA** FOX 1977
PERILOUS PASSAGE, THE Nicolayson, B.	**PASSAGE, THE** HEMDALE 1978
PRISONERS OF QUAI DONG, THE Kolpacoff, V.	**PHYSICAL ASSAULT** Titan 1973
PROCANE CHRONICLE, THE Bleeck, O.	**ST. IVES** COL—WAR 1976
RAINBIRD PATTERN, THE Canning, V.	**FAMILY PLOT** UN 1976

ORIGINAL TITLE	FILM TITLE
REPORT TO THE COMMISSIONER Mills, J.	**OPERATION UNDERCOVER** UN 1975
RESCUERS AND MISS BIANCA, THE Sharp, M.	**RESCUERS** DISNEY 1977
RIPLEY'S GAME Highsmith, P.	**AMERICAN FRIEND, THE** CINEGATE 1978
RUNNING SCARED Burmeister, J.	**TIGERS DON'T CRY** RANK 1978
SEVEN MEN AT DAYBREAK Burgess, A.	**OPERATION DAYBREAK** COL–WAR 1975
SHATTERED Dwyer, K.R.	**PASSENGERS** COL–WAR 1976
SIR, YOU BASTARD Newman, G.F.	**TAKE, THE** COL–WAR 1974
SIX DAYS OF THE CONDOR Grady, J.	**3 DAYS OF THE CONDOR** PAR 1975
SOMEONE IS KILLING THE GREAT CHEFS OF EUROPE Lyons, N. & Lyons, I.	**TOO MANY CHEFS** GTO 1979
SPORTING PROPOSITION, A Aldridge, J.	**RIDE A WILD PONY** DISNEY 1975
SYMBOL, THE Bessie, A.	**SEX SYMBOL, THE** WAR 1974
TEN SECOND JAILBREAK Asinof, E.	**BREAKOUT** COL–WAR 1975
TESS OF THE D'URBERVILLES Hardy, T.	**TESS** COL 1979
THORN BIRDS, THE McCullough, C.	**TIM** PISCES 1979
THREE MUSKETEERS, THE Dumas, A.	**FOUR MUSKETEERS, THE** FOX–RANK 1974

ORIGINAL TITLE	FILM TITLE
TO ELVIS WITH LOVE Canada, L.	**TOUCHED BY LOVE** COL 1980
TOM JONES Fielding, H.	**BAWDY ADVENTURES OF TOM JONES, THE** CIC 1976
TOUCH OF THE LION'S PAW, A Lambert, D.	**ROUGH CUT** PAR 1980
TOWER, THE Stern, R.M.	**TOWERING INFERNO, THE** COL—WAR 1975
TRUE GRIT Portis, C.	**ROOSTER COGBURN** UN 1975
VALLEY OF THE ANTS, THE Wells, H.G.	**EMPIRE OF THE ANTS** BRENT WALKER 1978
VIPER THREE Wager, W.	**TWILIGHT'S LAST GLEAMING** HEMDALE 1977
WAGES OF FEAR Arnaud, G.	**SORCERER, THE** CIC 1978
WATER IS WIDE, THE Conroy, P.	**CONRACK** FOX 1976
WHEEL SPINS, THE White, E.L.	**LADY VANISHES, THE** RANK 1979
WILLING FLESH Heinrich, W.	**CROSS OF IRON** EMI 1976
WINE AND THE MUSIC, THE Barrett, W.E.	**PIECES OF DREAMS** UA 1975
WONDERFUL WIZARD OF OZ, THE Baum, F.	**WIZ, THE** DISNEY 1979
YEAR OF THE BIG CAT, THE Dietz, L.	**RETURN OF THE BIG CAT** DISNEY 1974
YEKL Cahan, A.	**HESTER STREET** CONNOISSEUR 1975